# AT

# FIRST

# LIGHT

Strengthening
Buffalo Niagara
in the New Century

*Collected*
*Essays and Speeches*

## KEVIN P. GAUGHAN

**FOREWARD BY ROBERT F. KENNEDY, JR.**

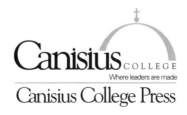

Canisius College Press

First published in the United States of America in 2003 by Canisius College Press

Copyright pending.

For more information, contact:
Canisius College Press
2001 Main Street
Buffalo, NY 14208


Publisher:      Joseph F. Bieron

Library of Congress
Catalog Card number pending

Layout Design:   Anne-Marie Dobies

Cover Photo:  Sharon Cantillon
Photo on Page 136: Robert Smith
All Other Photos: Thomas A. Wolf


ISBN 0 - 9740936 - 0 - 2
Printed in the United States of America

For my Mother

*November 23, 2004*

*For Scott,*

*A kind and generous community-giver, gifted businessman, empathetic spirit, and man in full.*

*With warm friendship and high esteem.*

*Ken P. Gu___*

# Table of
# CONTENTS

FOREWORD
By Robert F. Kennedy, Jr.

INTRODUCTION

ACKNOWLEDGMENTS

CHRONOLOGY OF PROJECTS

**REGIONALISM**
A Chautauqua Challenge: Save Our City; Save Our Souls          2
Wanted: Post-Chautauqua Bold Rush                             6
Regional Planning For Our New Century                         9
A Regional Report Card                                        12
Viewing Bush and Gore
    Through A Regional Looking Glass       15
Growing By Choice, Not By Chance                              17
Where To Now, Regionalism                                     19

**REFORM**
The Citizen Frank                                             28
Political Cents and Community Sensibility                     31
Must See T.V.                                                 34
Let's Send Political Ads Down Tobacco Road                    37
A Buffalo Constitutional Convention                           40
Peace Bridge Consensus Building                               43

**RACE**
Race, Reform, and Regional Thinking                           50
Buffalo Common Council Downsizing                             55

**REMEMBRANCES**
Thomas Jefferson and John Adams                               60
Michael Collins and Eamonn De Valera                          66
The American President in Buffalo                             72
Saint Patrick                                                 78
Presidential Debates                                          80
Father Baker                                                  82
Theodore Roosevelt in Buffalo                                 88

# Table of
# CONTENTS

**RENEWAL**
A Time to Heal                                               102
Waterfront Dreams and Casino Nightmares                      105
Saving Private and Public Buffalo                            108
At First Light: A New Century Beckons                        111
The Eleventh of September                                    115

**PERSONAL**
Robert Kennedy                                               120
World War and Baby Boomers                                   123
A Merry, Buffalo Christmas                                   126
Austin McCracken Fox                                         128
Eulogy for My Father                                         132

**SELECTED SPEECHES**
Chautauqua Conference on Regionalism
   Opening Address, June 1, 1997              138
Chautauqua Conference on Regionalism in Education
   Opening Address, October 27, 1999          141
Collaborative Leadership in the New Century
   November 30, 1999                          146
Buffalo State College Strategic Planning Conference
   Keynote Address, November 30, 2001         159

**BIBLIOGRAPHY**                                             168

# FOREWORD

Meeting our obligations as citizens in a democratic society has never been easy in America. Today, it's never been more difficult, nor more important that we do.

Changing notions of what it means to be an American, combined with increased duties we feel in every aspect of life, compel us to re-think civic virtue in a complex, more hazardous, and less understood world. Many Americans are responding to this challenge by turning their energy and ability toward their own locality and it's unique gifts. In so doing, they echo the founding impulse of those who constructed this nation one city and one community at a time.

Along with advancing economic justice, caring for our rapidly aging population, and securing our natural landscape, restoring vitality to America's urban centers is among this generation's primary tasks. We aren't the first to attempt these measures. If we succeed in sustaining our cities as viable social and economic entities, we won't be the last. But if we fail, future generations will want to know why.

In this age of dominant corporate power and emphasis on private gain, asserting individual spirit and achieving communal interests takes on even greater meaning. This book offers a framework for civic initiative, and shows one way to affect local policy through individual effort.

Kevin Gaughan's approach is unique in style, but his aim is common to all who care for their hometown. His is an American voice, a New York voice, and most of all, a Buffalo voice. It's one my family and I have been listening to for over thirty years, and never tire of. Reading his words, nor will you.

ROBERT F. KENNEDY, JR.
Pace University School of Law
White Plains, New York

# INTRODUCTION

On what must have been for them a rather uninspired day in 1996, the Erie County Legislature asked if I would consider overseeing local efforts to construct a new courthouse in downtown Buffalo. I was serving as their policy director at the time, looking for a challenge, and thinking of moving on.

The City of Buffalo, Erie County, and New York State had been at odds for over a decade as to who was responsible for renovating our courts, during which time they languished in disrepair. No one knew who should pay for what, let alone whether government had the means to finance any public works project. One legislator confessed that he saw no way to accomplish the task without increasing local taxes. And citing the lack of suburban support for urban projects, he ended his pitch by saying, "if you actually find a way to get this done, no one will thank you."

I immediately accepted, and set off on a journey of discovery.

I thought of the story of a young Harry Truman who, as county judge responsible for building a new courthouse in Kansas City, Missouri, took weekend drives around America to see other court systems. I traveled through New York, Pennsylvania, and Virginia to view the latest in public space architecture. In addition to looking at marble and stone, I spoke with government and community leaders in small towns and large cities, and asked them how they got along.

I found that local governments no longer communicated let alone cooperated among themselves for the common good. I saw how that breakdown affected not only constructing new courthouses, but every government function, from repairing roads and economic development to educating children and housing senior citizens. I learned that fragmented government reflects fragmented communities, and that the barriers of old and tired boundaries were imposing their harshest burden on inner city life.

And in trying to solve these problems, I came across the doctrine of regionalism.

I expanded my travel to successful American cities in Tennessee, Oregon, and North Carolina. Speaking with bright and innovative public servants, I learned of new collaborative practices to reform local governance and restore shared community across urban-suburban boundaries.

There exist several definitions of regionalism. But I've come to view it as just a fancy word for serving others, and aspiring to something larger than yourself. And in discovering regionalism through my courthouse efforts, I found my life's work, for which much that had come before had prepared me.

Among my most vivid memories of growing up in a family of seven children are dinnertime conversations. My father encouraged a somewhat British House of Commons practice in which anyone could speak at any time. In the ensuing mayhem and confusion that were family meals — my mother being the only one who emerged from that period with her dignity intact — it was only through the strength of your ideas and the mastery of your subject that you could hold the floor. It was our first lesson in the power of ideas, the importance of expressing yourself in clear manner, and the enriching nature of knowledge. And it was great fun.

But not always. As preparation for these gatherings, my father gave each of us weekly reading and writing assignments. We could select a book or newspaper article and every Saturday submit an essay that would shape our Sunday evening discussions. (I recall my sister Patricia, at age 8, producing a gripping review of "See Jane Run.") My father managed to keep these exercises interesting, but they lost much of their allure once you reached adolescence and developed other interests.

By that time, he'd connected us with the outside world in more direct manner. With his entrepreneurial efforts and government service taking him away much of the time, my father divided us into groups of two and took one group with him on virtually every trip. My brother Vincent and I were paired, and when our turn came around I was thrilled. When these trips coincided with school, my father would advise my principal or headmaster that I was with him and not to worry. Still, he'd make me duck down in the car when we'd pass a school bus on the way to the airport "just in case any truant officer was on the lookout."

We accompanied him to every meeting, conference, or social obligation he had, and were expected to be dressed and prepared for any occasion. Whether his work took him to a Los Angeles law office or a Capitol Hill chamber, he'd introduce us to each businessman, senator, or United States president he met, instruct us to take a seat, and encourage us to make notes on what we saw and learned.

There were some who didn't appreciate my father's spirit, and resisted our presence. But he paid them no mind. The larger and more broad-minded the man (there were too few women public servants then), the more they shared and engaged us. And from them we learned much. (I recall Estes Kefauver and my father running down a Capitol Hill hallway in pursuit of a constituent who had left the Tennessee senator's office just as we arrived. She was a survivor of the Titanic, and they wanted me to shake her hand.)

Through this unique gift, my father showed us that there were people who devoted their life to serving others; some for the right reasons, others less so. I came away, at an early age, able to distinguish between those interested in power, and those in service; full of admiration for those working for the public good; and convinced that someday perhaps I could contribute as well.

I also emerged comfortable speaking with and seeking assistance from anyone at anytime, no matter their position. The habit first revealed itself when I was a lowly intern at the U.S. Department of Justice in Washington during law school, and thought nothing of asking the Attorney General for help with an assignment. I remember it taking a while for him to get used to it.

Of course, my father never could have bestowed these gifts without my mother's guidance. She somehow sensed that knowing the outer world must be balanced by the inner strength of knowing yourself. My earliest memory is of her placing me on her lap on a spring afternoon, and reading to me in clear and nurturing voice as Lake Erie settled and robins and sparrows prepared for nightfall.

My father's work told us that as Americans we were part of a story that required our contribution. But my mother's behavior always reminded us that in any such restless journey, there is no place like home.

The practical power of that message came through my first year in college. Unable to sleep for the first several weeks, with some embarrassment I finally visited the student health service. The doctor performed a few tests, and just before moving onto more serious procedures, asked where I lived at home. When I said my bedroom overlooked Lake Erie, his eyes lit up. The next day he handed me an "8-track" recording of waves splashing on a beach and suggested I play it in the evening. After that, I was Cambridge's soundest sleeper.

So in 1996, when I realized that in my hometown local government was broken, that urban-suburban collaboration would create a region stronger than the sum of its fragmented parts, and that a national conference would best begin the process, it was second nature for me to ask local leaders to help, the Chautauqua Institution to host, national experts to speak, public officials to attend, and America's premier philanthropic organization, the Ford Foundation, to finance it.

I didn't think it would be at all difficult. Until I began. With political opposition from those who feared the conference and business resistance from those who wanted to control it, I immediately realized that my education in creating consensus for change had just begun.

I crafted my efforts in the form of conferences believing that they offer the most effective path to reform. But none of them — from the first regionalism gathering and the region-wide conversation, through the education conclaves and the Erie Canal public forum — have been just a conference. Rather, each one served as acknowledgment that a public policy was broken, and attempted to give community-wide voice to its repair. As such, they all reflected the new practices of inclusive governance and collaborative leadership.

And therein, as Shakespeare said, lay the rub. For these initiatives represent stark departure from old and closed processes that led to our shrinking economy and sunken spirit. And those with an interest in preserving present practices, it turns out, never go without a fight.

Rather than commit their same competitive mistakes, I've tried to harness the power of cooperative manner. Toward that end, I've spoken before more than a thousand community groups, conferences, college campuses, senior citizen centers, churches, and schools throughout Western New York and around America, and published some fifty essays.

The aim of every speech and essay has been to serve my work. Speaking invitations are an honor and, for me, a serious obligation. (No matter how prepared I am, my left leg still shakes, at times uncontrollably. I've learned to disguise it, but am open to any suggestion how to stop it.) In each instance, I came away learning more than I ever hoped to impart, and I'm always grateful to those who ask for copies of my remarks. Those requests are tributes to every teacher and professor who instilled in me a belief in the force of the spoken word.

As for the essays, as historian David McCullough has noted, taking pen to paper (or fingertips to keyboard) organizes your thoughts in a way unattainable though mere reflection. For me, writing is an act of self-discovery. You find out what you truly believe and hold dear. It's enriching, painful, and, somehow, magical.

The articles here that address regional reform and renewal I wrote to supplement my community work. The history pieces aim to convey the rich and unique contributions that Buffalo has made to the American narrative. Their added benefit was that doing archive research for them took my mind off setbacks to my pursuits. And I like to think that, along with my speaking efforts, they've helped advance the work.

I've attempted my civic service the only way I know how: with an enthusiasm born of love for Buffalo and Western New York. When I was a young boy, my father worried about my thin frame. Once a week, he'd lift me into a Radio Flyer wagon and pull me over to a neighbor physican's house for weighing. On the way home, I'd tell him stories. At the end of one long saga in which I'm sure he had little interest, he told me that my story was fair, but the enthusiasm with which I told it was without peer.

The word enthusiasm comes from three Greek words meaning "God in us," reflecting the ancient Greek's belief that when you were passionate about something, you were closest to the gods. My father was the most alive and impassioned person I have ever known. Enthusiasm for life and its endless opportunity is the most lasting gift he gave me.

When faced with the challenge of building a new courthouse in Buffalo, I knew the story of Harry Truman and his Missouri courts because years later as president, he brought the same imagination and will in overseeing renovation of the White House.

After its completion, Truman saved some material from the original White House and from it made courtroom gavels to symbolize his first elected office of county judge. Sufficient wood existed to make only a handful of gavels, one of which the president gave to my father. When I visit high schools, I take it along and have the students hold the same wood that perhaps John Adams, Abraham Lincoln, or Franklin Roosevelt touched.

Three American presidents turned to my father for advice. When he sought counsel, he turned to my mother. For this reason, and countless others, this book is dedicated to her.

KEVIN P. GAUGHAN
Buffalo, New York
April 21, 2003

# ACKNOWLEDGMENTS

All of my community efforts have been collaborations among individuals and institutions devoted to Buffalo Niagara. And none of the success with which they met would have been possible without their kindness and contributions.

I asked, encouraged, and, God help me, at times pestered individuals to take great risks to advance local reform. In the end, everyone I approached said yes; some willingly, others with reticence, but all with the joyous spirit that informs the Western New York character.

To insure wide range of opinion, and give as broad a swath as possible vested interest in their success, I crafted these initiatives in inclusive manner. By establishing a steering committee for each one — comprised of community leaders, lesser known achievers, and national experts in the profession — I assured wise counsel for them all.

In addition, I placed an institutional framework around each venture anchored by one nationally renowned entity — the Ford Foundation in the first regionalism conference, for example, or the National Trust for Historic Preservation with the Erie Canal forum. These acted as magnets for additional financing, and reassuring presence for those reluctant to join in.

How I was fortunate enough to prevail on Ford or the National Trust to engage in what they knew were controversial undertakings is perhaps the subject of a future book. Suffice it to say that persistence, a little imagination, a little more persistence, and a lot of luck don't hurt.

As for the Chautauqua Institution, it's a national treasure. And it's a local asset we've never effectively conveyed to the nation as part of our region. I've received some richly deserved ribbing for how the idea for the first conference occurred to me — returning home from the Institution one summer day, and unsettling other Thruway drivers as I simultaneously drove and jotted down notes. But the truth is I've always felt that we make too little use of this historic site. And I hope that young people will continue my work by placing more projects at Chautauqua.

Fostering collaboration among local governments proved difficult; among preservationists, dynamic; within the spiritual community, delightful; and among educators, a distinct pleasure. The human and intellectual capital with which our region is blessed is without parallel; and their generosity of spirit, without peer. The education I received working within each of these professions has made me a better Western New Yorker, a better American, and a better man.

Finally, as my father did for me, I included young people in every project, taking students along to meetings and strategy sessions in which I hope they learned something of value. As tomorrow's leaders, I know they'll do the same for the next generation.

Following is a list of projects and those who helped make them happen.

## CHAUTAUQUA CONFERENCE ON REGIONALISM

STEERING COMMITTEE: Stan Lundine, Dan Bratton, Judy Bloomquist, Sal Alfiero, Bill Greiner, Crystal Peoples, Mary Lou Rath, Lillian Ney, Henry Nowak, Seymour Knox IV, Leslie Braxton, Rich Tobe, Eva Hassett, Catherine Schweitzer, Gail Johnston, Robert Quintana, Ward Ewing, Carl Calabrese, Bob Wilmers, Jeff Swiatek, Carol Heckman, Dennis Mills, Laurie Dann, Neal Peirce, Bonnie Foit-Albert, Eras Bechakas, John Sheffer, Len Faulk, Rich Taczkowski, and Ed Yankelunas

SUPPORTED BY: The Ford Foundation, The Gebbie Foundation, SUNY at Buffalo, The Baird Foundation, Mark IV Foundation, M&T Bank, Stan Lundine, National Fuel Corporation, Frederick G. Pierce, Amherst Industrial Development Agency, The Paul J. Koessler Foundation, Catherine F. Schweitzer, and Paine Webber

## REGION-WIDE CONVERSATION

STEERING COMMITTEE: Rev. Stan Bratton, Rev. Butch Mazur, Imam Fajri Ansari, Rabbi Ronne Friedman, Patricia Greenspan, Rev. John Powell, Lana Benatovich, Rev. Tom Yorty, Rev. Jeff Carter, Rev. David Selzer, Most Rev. Henry Mansell, Rev. Susan Strouse, Rev. James Williams, Marlene Glickman, Halim Muhammad, Rev. Dr. David McKee, Rev. Pierre Albrecht-Carrie, Rev. Troy Bronner, Rabbi Charles Shalman, Rt. Rev. David Bowman, Rev. Peter Bridgford, Rev. Msgr. Robert Cunningham, Rev. James Lewis, Tina Vu, Rev. David Persons, Sandra Rifkin, Rev. Merle Showers, and Rev. Msgr. Jerry Sullivan

SUPPORTED BY: The John R. Oshei Foundation, The Buffalo Renaissance Foundation, The Baird Foundation, Fleet Bank, NA, The Balbach Family Foundation, Mrs. Margaret M. Gaughan, Ciminelli Development, John T. Rigas, Eric Mower & Associates, Hamilton Houston and Lownie, and Wendy Pierce

## CHAUTAUQUA CONFERENCE
## ON REGIONALISM IN EDUCATION

STEERING COMMITTEE: Tom Frey, Carol Lorenc, Stan Lundine, Dan Bratton, Len Faulk, Judy Bloomquist, Ted Hershberg, Don Ogilvie, Dick Redington, Tom Baker, Don Boswell, James Barker, Elaine Cryer, George Gates, Muriel Howard, Tracy Diina, Bob Bennett, Jillian Bowden, James Harris, Andrew Rudnick, Charlie Stoddart, Katie Vogt Schneider, John Sheffer, Bill Johnson, David Vanini, Adam Urbanski, Chris Jacobs, Phil Rumore, Anne Leary, Dick Nathan, Cara Rosenthal, Skip Meno, James Houghton, Judy Weidemann, Troy Bronner, Laurie Dann, Colleen Gooch, Paul Cole, Jeff Carter, Kevin Helfer, Jim Higgins, Gail Johnstone, Frank Pogue, Catherine Schweitzer, John Powell, and Ron Tomalis

SUPPORTED BY: The John R. Oshei Foundation, The Gebbie Foundation, The Baird Foundation, Mrs. John W. Koessler, Jr., SUNY Fredonia Center for Rural Development and Governance, SUNY at Buffalo Institute for Local Governance and Regional Growth

## FROM CONVERSATION TO COLLABORATION
*(follow-up to the education conference)*

STEERING COMMITTEE: Allison Hyde, Don Ogilvie, Jacqueline Paone, Ted Hershberg, Phil Rumore, Judy Weidemann, Gary Orfield, Charlie Stoddart, Elaine Cryer, Paul Buchanan, Marion Canedo, David Vanini

SUPPORTED BY: The Baird Foundation, The John R. Oishei Foundation, Erie 1 BOCES, Erie 2 BOCES, City of Buffalo School District, Education Fund for Greater Buffalo, The Bison Fund, Every Person Influences a Child, Albright-Knox Art Gallery

## CANAL CONVERSATION

STEERING COMMITTEE: Dianne Bennett, Wendy Nicholas, Luke Rich, Ted Lownie, Larry Rubin, Chip Greico, Kevin Cotrell, Susan Warren Russ, Bob Skerker, Paul Koessler, Muriel Howard, David Gerber, Tom Blanchard, Murray Light, Bob Shibley, Don Boswell, David Vanini, Catherine Schweitzer, Tim Tielman, Paul Redding, David Stebbins, Ben Gair, John Sheffer, John Gurtler, Tony Fryer, Elaine Cryer, Marty Anisman, Paul Buchanan, John Conlin, Laurie Dann, Mark Jackson

SUPPORTED BY: The National Trust for Historic Perservation, The Western New York Foundation, The Margaret L. Wendt Foundation, The Paul J. Koessler Foundation, The Balbach Family Foundation, The Baird Foundation, Fleet Bank, NA, Daemen College, Alpha Graphics, Spot Coffee

My indebtedness to colleagues and supporters is something I can never fully repay. The warmth and richness of these friendships make me the luckiest guy in Western New York:

Regional collaborators throughout America from whom I've learned it all: Gary Orfield, Ted Hershberg, Alan Altshuler, Bill Hudnut, Neal Peirce, David Rusk, Anita Summers, Jerry Benjamin, and Bill Dodge, as well as local regionalism leaders Henry Taylor and John Sheffer. And especially Michael Lipsky at the Ford Foundation and Wendy Nicholas of the National Trust for Historic Preservation, who graciously endured my refusal to accept no for an answer.

Community leaders Erkie Kailbourne, Bob Irwin, Bob Wilmers, Brenda McDuffie, Lou Verruto, Paul Koessler, Rit Moot, Welles Moot, Don Boswell, Sal Alfiero, Muriel Howard, Bob Kresse, Murray Light, whose company my father so enjoyed, Tom Baker, Jack Walsh, Jr., Mary Kent Prentice, Rich Tobe, Doug Bean, Carl Paladino, Frank Mesiah, John Larry, and especially Stan Lipsey, who was among the first to see some wisdom in convening the Chautauqua conferences.

Teachers and professors Doris Kearns Goodwin, Frank Friedel, David Herbert Donald, Ruth Jones, Ed Williams, Pat Moynihan, Dave Strachan, Bill Morris, John Finley, the magnificent Sue Schapiro, and Austin Fox, who I loved.

I am most grateful to Margaret Sullivan, editor and vice president of The Buffalo News, for graciously permitting re-publication of those essays that first appeared in the News. These articles enjoyed the benefit of careful editing by Jerry Goldberg and Mike Vogel, and before them, Barbara Ireland. My thanks as well to Jamie Moses and Artvoice, Jack Connors of Buffalo Business First, and Rochester Magazine, in which other essays printed here were first published.

Special thanks to The Annenberg Public Policy Center in Washington, DC, where I first presented the paper from which the essay on page 38 is excerpted. And to the University of Oklahoma Political Commercials Archives, where my 1994 live television broadcasts, discussed in the essay on page 35, are now on catalogue.

Susan Warren Russ and her board and staff at Leadership Buffalo, Clare Root and Cyndi Horrigan, have been generous collaborators, as have Working for Downtown, Leadership Niagara, Hodgson Russ, the League of Women Voters, Katherine Tarbell, Polly Ferguson, Joan Photiadis, Lyle Toohey, The New Millennium Group, Tracy Diina, VOICE Buffalo, Molly Quackenbush, and the Buffalo and Erie County Historical Society. Thanks to WNED and Al Wallach for their kindness with my LeadersSpeak.Now talk, Bill Ransom and John DiSciullo of WKBW-TV, Frank Pacella and "AM Buffalo" for their discussions of my conferences, and my friends at Adelphia "Crossroads,"

Pete Anderson, Dave Seyse, and Lynn Gibbons.

My conferences have been enriched with performances by Mary Ramsey, John Lombardo, 10,000 Maniacs, Barbara Levy Daniels, and the Buffalo Philharmonic Orchestra.

Long and cherished friends of my family, Bill Schapiro, Mary Koessler, Jim Phillips, without whom at times I wouldn't know where to turn, Irwin Cohen, John Kemmer, Paula and Jim DeMarco, Errol Daniels, Jack Becker, Wayne Wisbaum, and Cathy and Mike Battaglia, whose strength is an inspiration.

Chuck Schumer, the only public servant to say that he'd like to be a part of one of my projects.

Catherine Schweitzer, whose kindness is beyond measure, Stan Lundine, Western New York's finest public servant ever, and the heroic Charles Balbach, whose laughter always lifts.

Dearest friends, John Thornton, Joe Mattimore, Bill Graebner, and Dianne Bennett, whose counsel and kindred spirit I cherish. Beth, Sarah, Matthew, and Gregory. And the best writer in Western New York, who's also the best friend in the history of friendship.

Buffalo Niagara's most able and forgiving editor, Joe Bieron, its most talented book designer, Anne-Marie Dobies, and my publisher, Canisius College Press.

And a band of brothers and sisters who, at times, actually admit to associating with me, Carol Brothers, Brad Nagel, Cindy Abbott, David Vanini, Elaine Cryer, Eli Mundy, Dan Lukasiewicz, Alisa Lukasiewicz, Newell Nussbaumer, Gloria Brennan, Joan and Carl Jacobs, Laurie Dann, Joyce and John Scherer, Jack O'Donnell, Joe DeBergalis, Kay Murphy, Mike Galluch, Nate Neuman, John Gurtler, Mary Beth Popp, my Daemen College students, my administrative assistant, Diane Nash, and her husband, John.

Not unlike avenues and parkways throughout our region, the streets of heaven are lined with Buffalo angels, many of whom were mentors and friends. I miss them, and hope they look down with favor on our collective efforts to complete the work they began: Seymour Knox III, Burt Flickinger, Jack Koessler, Dick Wolfe, Mary Lou Vogt, Dave Koch, and the beloved Peggy Balbach. ❖

# CHRONOLOGY
## CIVIC AND COMMUNITY INITIATIVES

| PROJECT | DATE | RESULT |
|---|---|---|
| Chautauqua Conference On Regionalism Founder | June 1997 | Introduces regional reform, urban-suburban cooperation, and land use planning to Western New York; attracts 3,000 participants; results in increased consolidation of local services; fosters establishment of regional economic development, marketing, and cultural tourism entities; begins practice of government/ business/philanthropic collaboration for community renewal |
| Proposes Citizens Regional Planning Commission | September 1997 | First idea to address sprawl and re-direct investment into City of Buffalo; modeled on Portland, Oregon urban growth boundary |
| Proposes New York State hold Constitutional Convention In Buffalo | September 1997 | Begins community-wide discussion on importance of Albany statutory and regulatory reform to allow local governments to respond to new age of reduced public revenues |
| Region-Wide Conversation Founder | November 1998 | Program of inter-religious discussions to foster under-standing among urban and suburban residents; pairs city and suburban congregations for formal talks using set curriculum; over 200 congrega-tions participate; administered by the Network of Religious Communities; adopted by three American cities |

# CIVIC AND COMMUNITY INITIATIVES

| PROJECT | DATE | RESULT |
| --- | --- | --- |
| Proposes Erie County name change to Buffalo County | February 1999 | Seeks to affirm suburban economic dependency on successful urban core, and project the most recognizable identity to the world economy |
| Proposes National Brownfields Center | April 1999 | Creates awareness of importance of remediating Buffalo's former industrial sites to attract urban investment and reduce market pressures for suburban development |
| Chautauqua Conference on Regionalism in Education Founder | October 1999 | Gathers national experts on: standards-based reform; charter schools; equitable public financing methods; increasing classroom diversity; and reducing disparity of opportunity between city and suburban students; over 800 participants |
| Proposes a) single school district for Erie County, and b) Buffalo School District establish its own charter school | November 1999 | Erie County Association of School Boards undertakes formal study to consolidate districts, May, 2001; Buffalo School Board approves a charter school, August, 2002; and seeks extensive network of charter schools, March, 2003 |
| From Conversation To Collaboration | March 2000 | Collaboration with New York State and Erie County school board associations to apply cooperative principles of Chautauqua conference to Buffalo Niagara; WNY education community establishes a permanent Task Force on Collaboration, April, 2000 |

# CIVIC AND COMMUNITY INITIATIVES

| PROJECT | DATE | RESULT |
|---|---|---|
| Canal Conversation: Buffalo Inner Harbor Development and the Erie Canal Founder | September 2000 | Public forum with national experts on heritage and cultural tourism, waterfront development, and Erie Canal's western terminus; attracts 2,500 participants; helps convince New York State to abandon plans to bury the Commercial Slip, and create a history-based Erie Canal Harbor with public access to a restored Commercial Slip and surrounding streetscape |
| Proposes Regional Planning Council | March 2001 | Utilizing "smart-growth" principles, seeks to vest all land-use decisions for Erie and Niagara counties in citizen-based body; Buffalo Niagara Partnership and Erie County announce land use commission, January, 2003 |
| Proposes formal name for region: Buffalo Niagara | April 2001 | Gathers editors, publishers, and news directors of print and electronic media outlets; asks for uniform policy for references to the region; consensus reached on "Buffalo Niagara" |
| Proposes Regional Assistance Corporation | February 2002 | Modeled on Municipal Assistance Corporation that saved New York City in 1970's; creates financial incentive for urban reform by offering federally guaranteed loans to Buffalo in exchange for increased regional cooperation: would also re-formulate sales tax sharing to benefit towns throughout Erie County |

# THE TRULY GREAT

*By Stephen Spender*

I think continually of those who were truly great.
Who, from the womb, remembered the soul's history
Through corridors of light where the hours are suns,
Endless and singing.  Whose lovely ambition
Was that their lips, still touched with fire,
Should tell of the Spirit, clothed from head to foot in song.
And who hoarded from the Spring branches
The desires falling across their bodies like blossoms.

What is precious, is never to forget
The essential delight of the blood drawn from ageless springs
Breaking through rocks in worlds before our earth.
Never to deny its pleasure in the morning simple light
Nor its grave evening demand for love.
Never to allow gradually the traffic to smother
With noise and fog, the flowering of the Spirit.

Near the snow, near the sun, in the highest fields,
See how these names are feted by the waving grass
And by the streamers of white cloud
And whispers of wind in the listening sky.
The names of those who in their lives fought for life,
Who wore at their hearts the fire's centre.
Born of the sun, they traveled a short while toward the sun
And left the vivid air signed with their honor.

# REGIONALISM

## *Regionalism*

It is plain that the city is not determined merely by community of place and by the exchange of mutual protection from harm and of good offices. These things must, indeed, exist if there is to be a city, yet the existence of all of them does not at once constitute a city. There must be, both in households and families, a sharing of the good life, in a form at once complete and self-sufficient. ❖

ARISTOTLE

A community is like a ship. Everyone ought to be prepared to take the helm. ❖

HENRIK IBSEN

## EDITOR'S NOTE ❖

This first article was written as a prelude to the June 1997 conference held at the Chautauqua Institution that began the regionalism movement in Western New York. The author's opening remarks at this conference begin on page 138.

# A CHAUTAUQUA CHALLENGE:
# SAVE OUR CITY; SAVE OUR SOULS

May 1997

In a Toronto theater, the musical "Ragtime" celebrates an era one hundred years ago, when American cities were entire worlds, everything was new, and anything was possible. A century later, our urban centers are on the brink of disappearing.

Operating under governmental structures unchanged since the time of Joplin, telegraphs, and Model T's, regions such as Buffalo and Erie County struggle to sustain inner-city life; heal urban-suburban conflict; create economic and educational opportunity; and eliminate the two millstones of multiple governments and high taxes that burden efforts to establish sustainable society.

We're all too familiar with the afflictions we face. Over time and in pernicious manner, they have erased memories of Western New York's enormous gifts: rich and diverse human resources; magnificent natural and man-made landscapes; fertile agricultural lands; and the City of Buffalo's historic role in shaping our nation's destiny.

Against this backdrop, I thought it time that we convene as a community to re-examine and perhaps re-imagine our path, and at the same time demonstrate to our country and ourselves that stars still illuminate it.

And I thought we might conduct this conversation of ideas in one of our nation's most historic centers for learning, and one of our region's most cherished cultural assets, the Chautuaqua Institution.

The doctrine of regionalism, the topic of the Chautauqua Conference, rests on the assertion that areas like ours must enlarge its vision beyond political boundaries created over a century ago, and coordinate governmental practices among wider social, economic, and geographic spheres.

Perhaps most important, regional thinkers who shall address us at Chautauqua eloquently emphasize that a community and its culture is not something anyone owns, but rather something in which we all share and to which we are all responsible.

As we struggle to create the world's first multi-cultural society, this uniquely American idea of citizens' common past and linked future becomes ever more essential to our success. As a result, the definition of civic virtue, changed since the times of Jefferson and Lincoln, and Roosevelt, will yet again evolve into deeper and more complex duties.

In recent weeks, national publications have identified Western New York as the sole exception to an economic resurgence sweeping America. And not for the first time, our weak economy has imposed its harshest burden on those least able to bear it — inner-city residents.

Growing impoverishment and isolation of Buffalo' urban minorities — aided by state and local policies and enforced by separate political boundaries — has eroded our sense of community, diminished our humanity, and made us, somehow, a lesser people.

The Conference's four days will offer an opportunity for each of us to lower our voices, roll up our sleeves, and consider new ways to govern ourselves, increase life-sustaining employment, and affirm the type of people we aspire to be. But before we can lift ourselves, we must consider and comprehend those events and policies that now hold us down.

At Chautauqua, Anita Summers of Pennsylvania's Wharton School will remind suburban residents of their social and economic relationship with the inner city. Stanford economist Doug Henton will describe his ideas that have reduced taxation levels in regions around the world. Minnesota State Legislator Myron Orfield will sketch housing and land use policies that reduce rudderless growth and enhance racial equality. And Harvard University's Alan Altshuler will assert the imperative of government consolidation.

Echoing the Talmud's plea, "if not us, who; if not now, when" a current teen-aged pop music composer asks, "Who will save your soul, if you won't save your own?"

While our parents and grandparents waged World War or endured Great Depression to save theirs, our task is perhaps less dramatic. But those who generations ago bartered their pride or gave their life to create a just and free society would be the first to insist that we embrace the challenge.

Informed by that most singular American virtue — eternal experiment — and our tradition of advancing shared interests through the test and exchange of ideas, the Chautauqua Conference will provide an opportunity to examine the fundamental relationship in American government: that between citizen and local representative.

And for Buffalo and Erie County to show America the way will be fitting and proper payment to those who a century ago made ours one of the world's leading regions; and as well discharge our duty to those who follow in the more inclusive and tolerant community we leave behind.

In his first inaugural address, President George Washington ascribed the creation of our democratic experiment to "the tranquil deliberations and voluntary consent of so many distinct communities." As we continue to live and seek to improve that experiment, we hope you will join in these "tranquil deliberations" at Chautauqua. ❖

## EDITOR'S NOTE ❖

Six articles on regionalism, written over a period from July, 1997 (immediately following the first Chautauqua Conference) to March, 2003 are presented here. The common theme of regionalism is addressed from various perspectives.

# Wanted: Post-Chautauqua Bold Rush _____ July 1997

Every idea, Oliver Wendell Holmes wrote, is an incitement. Yet until last month's Chautauqua Conference on Regional Governance, I never realized the lengths to which an idea can stir.

While crafting the Conference, my hope was that exposing citizens to new theories of governing, creating life-sustaining jobs, and dismantling social and racial barriers, might aid our search for a more prosperous community. I never dreamed that we would embrace these notions with enthusiasm — and even joy.

If Chautauqua showed anything, it's that Western New Yorkers yearn for, need, and now demand bold initiatives. And in the weeks since the gathering, they've gone to imaginative lengths to prove it to me.

My favorite was a motorist whose passion for regional governance overtook his good sense. Passing me on Delaware Avenue one morning, he pulled half his body out of his car and urged in (how shall I put it) colorful terms that change happen now. Only repeated assurances that we would try prodded him back inside his moving vehicle.

People stop me on the street, willing to offer their thoughts on Chautauqua and, almost inevitably, excitedly add their own ideas. In this age of ho-hum acceptance of government mediocrity, clearly something intriguing is at work.

Then there's the letters, brimming with interest and ideas. Some come with gifts. One person even sent a batch of delicious chocolate chip cookies.

The message is clear: The idea of regional cooperation has struck a chord. We must transform our region from a poster child for fragmented government to a community model of efficiency, collaboration, and tolerance.

To the degree that Chautauqua made us re-call our shared interests and re-affirm our linked futures, it was worthwhile. To the extent that it compels our public servants to act in more collaborative and cooperative manner, it's

❖

encouraging. But only by the amount of real reform it produces, shall the conference be judged a success.

For too long, the primary colors in local political thought have been strictly pastels, with no bold strokes sketching vivid hues. Caution bordering on fear has reduced policy offerings of elected officials to mush, and whenever they speak, all we hear, in George Gershwin's phrase, is blah blah blah blah blah. The resultant cynicism is growing old.

So it was exhilarating to have scholars and practitioners of regional coop-eration valiantly urge us to roll up our sleeves, re-discover meaning in our system of self-government, and re-affirm the type of people we aspire to be.

Having learned from them now, and seen the benefits that inure to regions that take control, our orders are clear. We need to march brave.

Upstate New York continues as the sole exception to an economic resurgence sweeping America, and not for the first time our weak economy imposes its harshest burden on those inner-city residents least able to bear it.

Growing impoverishment and isolation of Buffalo's urban minorities — aided by state and local policies and enforced by separate political bound-aries – has eroded our sense of community, diminished our humanity, and made us, somehow, a lesser people. It takes no policy wonk to see that intrepid thinking is required. We need:

- Land use concepts that both breathe new life into our city and preserve rural assets.
- Housing practices that foster increased contact among us.
- Government consolidations that reflect reality and vest elected officials with moral authority to ask sacrifice from the rest of us.
- Public education funding equitable to all.
- And state constitutional changes that ease adoption of all of the above.

And it takes no genius to know that we are equal to the task. But it will take more than politicians. Informed by the American tradition of citizen-led reform, regionalism calls upon each of us to have no fear, believe in ourselves and each other, and have faith in the magic of democracy.

I know what you're thinking: We've trusted before, and been betrayed. But if marriage after divorce, as Samuel Johnson said, is the triumph of hope over experience, then periodical renewal of democratic spirit, even after we've been knocked around a bit, is the American way.

The Chautuaqua Conference revealed one more enduring truth. Under our present layer of skepticism over government lies a uniquely American idealism ready once again to be tapped.

In the exuberant driver on Delaware Avenue, the cookies, and inspiring encounters with citizens willing to risk, I hear, taste, and feel a readiness to once again celebrate our democratic experiment, and take pride in our region and how we govern it.

Perhaps the same combination of skepticism and looming heroic deeds moved Thomas Jefferson some 221 years ago to lament the lack of courage in colonial public life before the American Revolution.

While preparing the Declaration of Independence, he wrote a friend that he was tired of living in an age in which, when it came to ways of governing, there was "nothing new under the sun." If he could get his colleagues to go for some of the radical concepts he was inserting in the document, Jefferson wrote, no one could ever say that again. ❖

# REGIONAL PLANNING FOR OUR NEW CENTURY——————April 1998

Spring of '98 brought increased pressure to grow Western New York's economy. Our leading employer and economic engine had rusted and quit decades ago. Newspaper reports noted that while most of America flourished in a new economic age, Erie County jobs and population continued downward.

A prominent Buffalo attorney began meeting secretly with an out-of-town businessman looking for a new base of operations. If we embraced his rapidly growing industry, the outsider promised, our region would enjoy increased employment, economic stability, a wider tax base, and larger public coffers. All he asked was a prime water location near the majesty of Niagara Falls, and some local investors to share the risk.

Sounds like 1998's lure of casino gambling. But the year was 1898, the Buffalo entrepreneur was John Milburn, and his outside partner was Walter Scranton, owner of the Lackawanna Iron and Steel Corporation of Scranton, Pennsylvania.

In the wake of a mid-1890's depression, Milburn knew that our days as a commercial trade center were numbered. The Erie Canal was 70 years old, new routes west were already imaginable, and an industrial future beckoned. And Scranton pined not for the natural wonder of the Falls, but for its cheap power to fuel steel mills the size of which many Americans had never seen.

Milburn and Scranton culminated their courtship over a Buffalo Club dinner on July 4, 1899. With one handshake, they transformed Buffalo into a steel town, employed several generations, enabled countless young summer workers to finance college, blackened the lungs of many more sent to an early grave, and defined Western New York's character and image for a century. In the process, they destroyed a glorious portion of pristine waterfront.

As pubic revenue producers, Lackawanna Steel and its successor Bethlehem

Steel proved problematic. Scranton insisted on a site within reach of Buffalo's public transportation but beyond the grasp of its taxation powers. Because the Town of West Seneca imposed virtually no property taxes, its lakefront parcel was ideal.

After only 6 years, though, town officials grew weary of the industry's dual burdens of expensive infrastructure and medical costs born of impoverished immigrants living in unsanitary conditions. "Steel germs" described not only the epidemic of typhoid fever that broke out in 1903, but as well steel's economic and social burden weighing on West Seneca's small government.

Southtowns businessmen realized, too, that the plant's presence was turning residential growth patterns north — leading swamps and wetlands to be transformed into the towns of Amherst and Clarence. Local elected officials finally petitioned the State legislature, and in 1909 the City of Lackawanna was incorporated, giving steel its own town.

As we face a new century, yet again striving for sustainable growth and inclusive community, the lessons of this hundred-year old story resonate. All too familiar elements exist: private decisions without public input; less-than-thoughtful consideration of both favorable and unfavorable aspects of the business; hyped short-term gain giving way to long-term harsh reality; and insufficient planning to maximize benefits, minimize burdens, and anticipate growth patterns resulting from the industry's arrival.

Region-wide planning would have addressed many of these pitfalls. And before we turn Western New York into Planet Casino — or before we derive our identity from any major enterprise — we owe it to ourselves and to posterity to form a citizens-based regional planning body. To grow by chance and not by choice is no longer viable in a cutthroat global market bent on winnowing competition and finishing off a struggling region such as ours.

An Erie-Niagara Planning Board, authorized by State law and indeed in existence in the 1980's, would provide for citizens, developers, real estate experts, farmers, and architects to craft and organize a comprehensive plan for our new century. Planners could encourage urban investment, determine which suburban centers we should enhance, and what natural and agricultural resources we can protect.

Our planning body might also nurture consensus on the character and image we wish to convey in the next hundred years. And that may prove handy as we consider the gaming industry. Think of the growing gambling addiction among teenagers, competition from internet casinos and now Fort Erie slot machines, and the blight surrounding several cities that recently turned to casinos. We may be taking on an idea whose time has passed.

Portland, Charlotte, Cleveland, and Pittsburgh are successful cities, and each of them has a regional planning entity that crosses political boundaries to unite development and marketing efforts. All have undergone sweeping, citizen-led analysis of what they offer and stand for. But none of them possess a God-given and man-made landscape that can hold a candle to Western New York.

A regional planning board will assure that future economic development expresses our social and cultural aspirations. Long after our national fascination with games of chance ends, that which renders our city and region unique shall remain. And by keeping history's lessons in our minds, Western New York planning and development can affirm this essential truth. ❖

# A REGIONAL REPORT CARD:
# "A" FOR PROGRESS; "C" FOR PACE

June 2000

Emerging now from our winter of discontent, stymied by debate over bridges and zoos, canals and convention centers, we do well to consider how far we've come in creating a vibrant region and restoring shared community, and how much work remains.

First, remember that context is everything. And the backdrop against which reform efforts take place are rapidly changing roles. Shelley wrote long ago that "poets are the unacknowledged legislators of the world." Today, citizens are.

Politicians rarely take public positions on matters anymore. Philanthropic organizations fill that vacuum by both funding and asserting programs and policy. The business community no longer assails public servants, but now engages them. And perhaps most important, citizens are re-defining the notion of community.

This sea change in the manner in which public policy consensus is created has skewered any sense of progress. But be neither discouraged nor disheartened, for our progress is real.

In the lexicon of regional thinking, two words appear in bold face: collaboration and inclusion. By both measures, we've grown. In the past three years, local government cooperation in purchasing, service delivery, and public safety has increased. While city and towns once sued one another over poaching companies, today a new county executive vows to consolidate area development agencies. And in the all-important marketing field, we finally have a financially strong and regionally aware private enterprise that's pitching us to the world.

Our Achilles heels remain land use planning and education. Unless we establish a regional planning board, prospects for encouraging urban investment and insuring sustainable suburban growth are slim. And until we increase collaboration among urban and suburban schools, chances for resuscitating Buffalo are none.

As for inclusion — making the decision-making table larger, less white-male, and more round — like an adolescent suddenly overcome by hormones and gangly limbs, rapid maturity has followed years of little change. And like that teenager, awkwardly we lurch, with growing pains that make us question whether growing up was worth the wait. It may not seem so to us. To future generations, it will.

Because those who assert that debating without advancing projects is harmful have it only partly right. They aim at too low a horizon, and think of too soon a generation. They don't see that responsibility for serving the common good is passing to a generation willing to sacrifice short-term gratification for long-term gain.

Nor do they understand that in this new age of inclusive governance among diverse peoples, there is no such thing as public outcry coming too late. However and whenever public awareness develops, it defines public interest.

The death of political bosses long ago, and the more recent demise of civic life being driven by a bunch of white guys at The Buffalo Club, guaranteed that this new day would come. And its arrival is a good thing.

With no memory of steel-mill smoke or urban unrest, these young community leaders also possess fierce pride in Buffalo, and even fiercer pride in any characteristic that renders it unique. A soaring bridge or restored Erie Canal are thus matters for which they will go to the barricades.

Our task is to remind them that there is life somewhere beyond those barricades, that it holds promise beyond measure, and that we must now find our way there.

That will require collaborative leadership, willingness to permit ideal aspirations to meet political reality, and gritty determination to work through our nascent renewal, knowing that vast rewards await those who persevere.

Like Estragon in Samuel Beckett's "Waiting for Godot," weary Western New Yorkers may feel that "we can't go on like this." But we must recall

Vladimir's bold and fearless response, "that's what you think."

We know that every harsh winter is followed by a new birth of spring, with all the promise that season evokes. And we must remember that by holding firm to the practices of inclusive governance, we will someday soon greet the spring as one. ❖

# VIEWING BUSH AND GORE THROUGH
# A REGIONAL LOOKING GLASS___October 2000

In addition to the complex matters that all Americans should weigh in deciding who gets our presidential vote, Western New Yorkers must add another one.

Ours is an issue less heart-wrenching than women's choice, less confusing than targeted tax cuts, less obvious than senior citizen prescription drugs, but no less important than any of them.

It's the question of how the next president will assist struggling urban centers like Buffalo in the rapidly approaching post-suburban age. And perhaps more than any other American city, we should have clear understanding of both candidates' views.

Regional thinking seeks to resuscitate cities through more equitable sharing of resources and responsibilities among urban and suburban areas. Innovations include regional planning to increase urban investment and reduce suburban sprawl; attacking education inequity with city-suburban school collaboration; consolidating overlapping government bureaucracies; and transportation policies that join urban workforces with suburban jobs.

At campaign's start, Al Gore asserted that addressing sprawl would be among his most urgent tasks. But his initial ardor quickly dissolved into amorphous discussions of "livability." He captured suburbanites' disdain for traffic jams, but missed the original purpose of reversing sprawl, that of redirecting resources toward the city.

As for George W. Bush, I never heard him utter the words region, sprawl, or planning; except for "government planning," a phrase he spit out while doing everything but holding his nose.

None of the three presidential debates included an urban policy discussion let alone analysis of the American city's role in the new century. And with regions increasingly recognizing the essential part that cities and their unique history, architecture, and sense of place play in our future, we shall regret this gaping hole.

And here's why. Even if both candidates overstate future government surpluses, new technology will continue to produce unfathomable wealth. As society continues to redefine notions of humane behavior, we'll recognize the inhumanity of people living in urban poverty a stone's throw away from comfortable suburban affluence. And perhaps that evolution will coincide with sufficient public resources with which to address it.

Not long ago, we breathed cancerous smoke on one another in public, banned handicapped people from events for lack of access, and quietly turned our back on sexual harassment. Just as a few bold individuals overcame resistance and ended those practices, some courageous cities and regions will reduce the disparity of opportunity that haunts the American urban experience. And they will be tomorrow's success stories.

Not only should Buffalo be among them, we should be first among them. And we should expect innovative federal programs to assist us in the effort.

In our last socially-aware and affluent era of the 1960's, we learned that while we cannot erase poverty, we can change its face. Today, inner-city Americans of color suffer more the impoverishment of isolation than of dire economic straits. They feel more remote and less American. And they seek uniting policies that dismantle barriers to entry into a more vibrant and less desolate world.

While our presidential candidates remained silent, Congress has added new eligibility requirements for certain federal funds. New legislation now makes urban-suburban collaboration a prerequisite for many federal programs. In some instances, philanthropic organizations and surrounding suburbs must join a city's grant application to be successful.

At the very least, these innovations should be further expanded to encourage regional cooperation and affirm the wisdom of joining city and suburb to strengthen each. And the presidential candidate who advances this notion deserves our support. ❖

# GROWING BY CHOICE, NOT CHANCE

March 2001

Close your eyes and picture any attractive American urban setting. Boston's colonial Back Bay, hugging the Charles River; New York's bucolic Gramercy Park, nestled among nearby commercial strips; or San Francisco's stunning Nob Hill, its residential pattern mirroring nearby natural landscape.

Contrast those images with the sullen and soulless environs we've come to know as suburbs. Roads like airport runways, lined by bland, interchangeable boxes masquerading as architecture, and set behind endless concrete parking lots where pedestrian walkways should be.

The difference? Each city neighborhood is a product of comprehensive design undertaken by cooperative urban leaders. Indeed, every functional and appealing American city you can summon to mind — including Joseph Ellicott's Paris-based grid fused with Frederick Law Olmsted's green in Buffalo — was born of organized, collaborative planning.

As for our suburbs, they are a mishmash of unplanned growth. The product of fragmented decisions made during an exploding suburban age when public funds existed to both sustain cities and support urban flight, suburbs are an American dysfunction. They helped cause our nation's unique blend of cultures to cease melting, and begin severing. And with the exception of village centers designed to sustain original sense of place, they're about to become worse.

Today, individual town planning is done without regard to, let alone communication with, other localities. So savvy developers play suburb against suburb in a quest to obtain favorable arrangements. And as we recently saw along the Amherst /Cheektowaga border, one result is yet another large retail box almost slipping into an area where three others already exist.

Another is water, electricity, roads, and other infrastructure extending further and further into our natural habitat at taxpayers' expense.

In 1960, Buffalo-Niagara's 1,054,000 residents lived on 162 square miles of land. By 1990, our reduced population of 954,00 sprawled over 286 square miles. Over 30 years, we lost 9% of our people while we developed 76% more land.

We can continue on this path of growing by chance and not by choice, and hold little hope of increasing urban investment and crafting sustainable suburban growth. Or we can apply those cooperative practices which blended form with function in our city throughout the region, and make collaborative decisions about where behemoth retail boxes can sit, and on what bucolic settings we'll take our stand.

That's why I've proposed establishment of a Buffalo Niagara Regional Planning Council, a citizens-based panel to devise development policies throughout Erie and Niagara counties, encourage investment in Buffalo and Niagara Falls, and inform local planning decisions with regional purpose.

Opponents say that government planning would stifle development. But regional planning seeks not to thwart growth, but to organize it in sustainable manner. The question is not whether to grow, but how. How do we insure that new development will add value to existing neighborhoods, enhance quality of life, and advance a coordinated, regional purpose. An entity that considers the effect of Cheetowaga's decisions on Amherst, and Amherst's on Buffalo, will go a long way toward achieving that end.

The sticky wicket is regional planning's effect on local governments' traditional role in overseeing their own affairs. Reconciling individual towns' right to regulate growth with the responsibility we all share to a larger, regional purpose, is a delicate balance. But one that can be achieved, especially if counties lead by example and acknowledge that regionalism requires thinking beyond even county borders.

"Too low they build who build beneath the stars," asserted Greek historian Thucydides. Through proper planning, a vibrant region that captures the nation's imagination and the attention of those who seek full and enriching lives, is a star within our grasp. ❖

# WHERE TO NOW, REGIONALISM?

March, 2003

Late in his long life, founding father John Adams had a favorite story he told to illustrate the spirit that informed the American Revolution and contributed to its success.

Throughout Adams' efforts to persuade colonialists to sever ties with England, his chief opponent was John Dickinson of Pennsylvania. From the late 1760's right up to the decisive vote to declare independence, Dickinson argued for reconciliation with Britain, and maintenance of a status quo that had rendered him among Pennsylvania's most affluent figures. Feeling his convictions deeply, Dickinson ceased speaking with Adams and, in the end, couldn't bring himself to attend the July 1776 session in which the Continental Congress made its fateful break.

But as Adams loved to tell it, at 7:00 am the morning after the Declaration of Independence was signed, a Pennsylvania militia marched out of Philadelphia to defend the infant nation. At its head stood John Dickinson. And as he marched passed Adams tipping his hat, Adams, deeply moved, said, "there goes an American spirit no other nation will ever match."

Unfortunately, as public debate over regional reform and the future of Buffalo grows more intense, few politicians have reached for the future the way Americans of 1776 did. To the contrary, those opposed to breaking with the past have successfully beaten back new ideas out of fear and, at times, self-interest.

But with Mayor Masiello's recent acknowledgment of the inevitability of change, we've reached a threshold. Like those heroic Americans who took us from colonies to colossus, we have entered an age of experiment. And to vest those who've resisted reform with the same spirit with which John Dickinson embraced freedom, regional thinkers must now set a realistic course to universal benefits for all Western New Yorkers.

We must build a coalition in support of reducing government to increase opportunity. That can only be accomplished by combining present emphasis on efficiency-based reforms with wider support for equity-seeking change. In other words, producing less government will never be achieved without enhancing community fairness. And before we begin combining local governments, we must first reduce their size.

## WHERE WE ARE

As it turns out, necessity truly is the mother of invention. By any measure, Buffalo's financial crisis is beyond the resolution of any approach short of revolutionary. Further cutting sidewalk repair or parks maintenance funds will not fill a $38 million financial hole.

City schools brim with impoverished students, many of whom require special education services and most of whom sit in facilities that can't hold a candle to suburban schools. And yet again, Buffalo's superintendent prepares to send teachers home. As for human services, Buffalo long ago lost its ability to provide innovative assistance to those least able to fend for themselves.

But the impetus for change doesn't stop there. Add a bloated state government whose stubborn adherence to broken practices today squeezes state legislators between ending pre-school for four-year olds and reducing medical care for the poor.

And finally, mix in a federal government poised to wage war and plunge its budget into long-term deficits. It's clear that the answer to our local financial crises must lie not in Albany or Washington, but rather in ourselves.

## WHERE WE'RE HEADED

Merging Buffalo and Erie County is not inevitable. But here's what is: the structure and appearance of local governments throughout America is about to drastically change. City and suburban political boundaries have lost any relation to social and economic challenges facing localities. And those

20

America cities that act on that reality will anchor flourishing regions.

As the sole American level of government that remains unreformed in the post-modern age, local government has been "biggie-sizing" itself long before the trend reached fast food emporiums.

Consider recent discussions of merging the offices of Buffalo City Comptroller and Erie County Comptroller. Erie County immediately asserted that its financial offices could discharge Buffalo's comptroller duties with little adjustment. No one posed the obvious question that if the County Comptroller's staff of almost 60 employees could discharge the functions of an additional municipality, what's keeping them busy today?

Do we really need almost 60 county comptroller employees, let alone 36 more in Buffalo's finance office? An informal survey of a half dozen large Western New York companies reveals a much smaller ratio of comptroller-employees to total employees. Indeed, one corporation acknowledged that if it had the same ratio of comptroller-employees to total employees as the City of Buffalo, their comptrollers office would triple in size.

Thus, while Mayor Maisello and Erie County Executive Giambra now loudly proclaim agreement on consolidation, they remain silent partners in failing to cut their governments to prepare for such a change. As a result, the reform movement is vulnerable to reminders of the effects of stones on glass houses.

Recent discussions of the relationship of our mayor and county executive capture the importance of government leaders' role in reform, but miss those shortcomings that impair their respective abilities to effect it.

As the leading government spokesperson for consolidation, Giambra champions the important aim of reducing broad tax burdens that weigh on our community's narrow shoulders. But his silence on regionalism's other missions undermine his ability to create consensus for structural change.

A basic tenet of regional thinking is you must always make the table larger. Which means, if you want others to favor your notion of change, you must support theirs. By this method, leaders create coalitions whose interests at least partially overlap.

❖

Giambra's assertion that sprawl (defined as suburban development without region-wide population growth) does not exist in Buffalo Niagara cuts him off from a large sector of regionalists. So, too, his disdain for progressive tax sharing and housing and public transportation reforms.

Masiello's inability to connect regional reform with long-term benefits for our city has been regrettable. While the recent agreement with the police union is promising, until he grasps regionalism's main purpose of reviving city investment, the mayor will appear interested merely in short-term budget balancing.

But most important, both officials are silent on the largest impediment to structural reform: its perceived effect on inner city people of color, who view consolidation as a reduction of their political influence.

## START BY ENLARGING THE CITY

To begin constructive discussion of refashioning local government, here's a broad-stroke outline of what a Buffalo Metropolitan Government — "BMG" — might look like. This model assumes that New York agrees to temporarily exempt our region from those state laws that today prohibit these measures.

Any government re-structuring plan must bear one harsh reality in mind: the only boundary that holds any political meaning in America today is a city-suburban one. It purports to define racial and economic differences in constituencies, and sadly remains a powerful basis on which a politician makes decisions.

Viewed through this prism, any politician concludes that with less than one-third of constituents living in Buffalo, resources should be allocated to satisfy the two-thirds suburban population. But to succeed, a new, consolidated BMG must in the end strengthen the city, and ensure that the voice of its most vulnerable residents is not reduced. A new region-wide legislative body, then, must have a majority of its members represent the urban core.

As Buffalo's population does not today merit that, step one is to merge the city with those inner-ring suburbs that share certain of its challenges, perhaps Lackawanna, Cheektowaga, and West Seneca. Residents of this newly-enlarged Buffalo would then comprise more than 50% of Erie County's total population.

As a result, after the second step of city-county merger, a majority of BMG's new legislature would represent the urban core. Envision an eleven-member body, for example, with six members representing the (new) city, and five coming from the suburbs.

Simultaneous with BMG's creation, all town boards and village municipalities throughout Erie County would be abolished. The office of county executive and its departments would preside, with Buffalo's mayor and town superintendents continuing as accountable executives in their respective jurisdictions.

## A GAME PLAN

How do we get there from here? First, political leaders must provide direction and purpose to reform, connecting the dots of less government with the lines of economic opportunity for all. Even George W. Bush recognizes the emptiness of conservative change if it doesn't lead to compassionate choices.

Second, politicians must press harder for collaborative initiatives today within our grasp, if only to get a few tangible triumphs under our belt. Momentum from even small changes will produce what sailors call "apparent wind" — favorable breeze that hits only those vessels in motion, and allow them to reach their destination faster.

The federal government can encourage our experimental age. Senator Charles Schumer's recent proposal for one-time Washington grants to struggling municipalities throughout America, if adopted, should go only to local governments undertaking consolidation and collaborative measures.

Erie County, Buffalo, and local philanthropic organizations should consider retaining an outside consultant to put some flesh on the bare bones described here. The Brookings Institution acted as formal advisor to Louis-ville, Kentucky, guiding that region through seemingly insurmountable legal and political obstacles to its new streamlined government. We're ready now for comparable advice.

Finally, and as a symbolic gesture, it's time to change Erie County's name to Buffalo County. Two years ago, the City of Ottawa, Canada merged with eight surrounding regional governments. The new government adopted Ottawa as its name, knowing it was the identity most recognized around the world. In a Buffalo County, there'd be no question of who we are, what we value, and to what we as a region are committed. ❖

# REFORM

## *Reform*

As life is action and passion, it is required of a man that he should share the action and passion of his time, at peril of being judged not to have lived. ❖
                    OLIVER WENDELL HOLMES

There is nothing permanent except change.❖
                    HERACLITUS

## EDITOR'S NOTE ❖

The articles in this chapter draw on the author's experiences as a candidate for public office and an advocate for better government, to make thought provoking recommendations for change.

# THE CITIZEN FRANK —————————————April 1992

America faces a critical decision concerning its postal service that affects as well the integrity of its public servants. And the answer is neither a young Elvis nor old, but rather, you.

In accordance with a privilege granted them by the first Continental Congress, our U.S. senators and representatives are gearing up this election year to expropriate more than $135 million of taxpayers funds to pay for hard sell, direct mail advertising of themselves.

With the exception of a brief 19th century spell of what Emerson called "the anxiety of influence" (from which they quickly recovered), Congress has used the "frank" — meaning free from the Franks or free men of Gaul, who comprised the ruling elite — as mail order pork.

Indeed, that which Congress will spend this year on free mail alone will far exceed the amount they allocated to re-build Western New York roads for a generation to come.

The original intent of the 18th century law permitting congressmen free use of the postal service was to spare representatives the cost of responding to constituents' written inquiries.

Never in their wildest dreams did the Founding Fathers envision that their bill would someday result in truckloads of bulk mailings of 100,000 to 300,000 pieces per mailing to unsuspecting citizens at a cost to taxpayers of 47 cents per piece.

The House Franking Commission makes two assertions in support of the privilege:

- Taxpayer-financed direct mail is the only effective means to communicate with more than 3000,000 households in a district.

- Constituents have a right to notice of "town meeting" forums held by their representative.

The former contention is relevant, but not true, and the latter true, but not relevant.

Taking the household argument to its logical conclusion would require Senator Pat Moynihan, for example, to spend $10 million of public funds to communicate with his New York constituency, and President Bush more than $125 million to speak with his.

The fact is, as with any other profession, if you perform your duties well, those who depend on you will know it.

With respect to public meetings or hearings that a congressman schedules, they can be and are publicized by print and electronic media, and computers, with no cost to taxpayers.

Frankly, congressional insistence that the present system is cost efficient is like Phil Donahue attempting to impersonate Mick Jagger — plenty of effort, but no effect.

I propose an alternative that will both reverse ascendant cynicism about public service, reduce our crippling deficit, and in a small yet profound manner, return a portion of government to people.

- Abolish the franking privilege for all members of Congress.

- Grant each American a "citizen frank" by which he or she may 12 times per year address written questions or comments to congressman at no cost.

- Twelve pre-printed envelopes with corner space for citizens' signatures may be obtained in January of each year at a local congressional district office.

- Attached to each citizen envelope would be a return envelope by which the representative could borrow his or her constituent's privilege to respond to the initial letter. In other words, the privilege would vest in citizens who, at their discretion, may up to once per month extend the benefit to their representative for the purpose of response.

- Corporations or other collective entities would be entitled to 6 citizen franks per year.

The House Franking Commission, an already existing body, would implement and oversee this procedure at a savings to taxpayers of more than $100 million annually.

If this proposal sounds like an idealistic appeal to what Abraham Lincoln called the better angels of our nature, it is. But its simplicity belies its importance.

America is a shared affirmation of ideas. But today, it's difficult to hear the sound of our soul over the din of petty and partisan politics. In the end, a citizen frank would replace the heavy hand of government with the light touch of its citizens. A small accomplishment, that, but a good one. ❖

# POLITICAL CENTS AND
# COMMUNITY SENSIBLITY_____February 1996

A few summers ago, historian David McCullough asked a Chautauqua Institution audience why our generation had produced no monumental public works. Where was our age's gift to posterity, he challenged, our Metropolitan Museum of Art, Golden Gate Bridge, or other lasting symbol to be celebrated through time.

Returning home from New York City recently, McCullough's question still echoed. After explaining to state officials why Erie County's finances did not permit us a majestic new courthouse, I wondered whether we might never again create for the ages.

With tributes to ancient achievements rushing by below — Utica, Rome, and Syracuse — I lamented the irony of our state's financial plight: unable to sustain winter heating assistance to impoverished families, to preserve and enhance the natural resources of Lake Erie shores, let alone finance the restoration of our magnificent Old County Hall.

Like Sisyphus and his rock, local governments appear condemned to push their budgets toward balance, only to be rolled down into the red by rapidly increasing social needs. The burdensome puzzle of how to raise revenue without raising taxes weighs heavily on any initiative to meet our social let alone generational duties.

And yet, as public assets disappear, ever larger concentrations of capital swirl just out of reach, amassed by and expended on behalf of political candidates who seek public office. Indeed, the only American institution not downsizing today are political campaign committees, whose revenues and expenditures grow ever larger for the purchase of ever smaller, more negative advertisements.

With television costs as their excuse, political candidates continue to push the pulp fiction that they have no choice but to beg: "I need your check so that I can continue to advance your interests." The result is a million dollar congressional race here, a two million dollar county executive race there, while the federal government closes parks and counties close libraries. The irony, I suspect, is unintended.

Something has gone wrong. To right it, I propose that the New York State Election Law be amended to compel every candidate for public office — from U.S. Senator to town highway superintendent — to contribute two cents of every campaign dollar raised to a public trust. My measure would at once restore some economic if not social redeeming value to a damaged campaign system, and provide a revenue source to supplement diminishing public coffers.

Here's how it would work. Each of New York's 56 counties would establish a public trust, administered by three trustees appointed by local federal judges. Trust principal would be invested, and interest proceeds allocated, to fund public endeavors in accordance with local priorities.

Inasmuch as presidential candidates receive public funding, they'd be carved out of the law. But for self-financed Ross Perot-like candidates for any other office, the bill would require two cents or each dollar they spent.

Finally, candidates would contribute to the county trust in which their district lies, with statewide or multi-county candidates dividing their contributions on a per capita basis.

The trust would also accept private contributions. Wealthy, elderly individuals seeking favorable tax treatment could make bequests with the stipulation that the principal amount be returned to their grandchildren. The public would thus have use of their funds for a significant length of time, along with interest generated, and the contributor receives a nifty tax shelter.

If Erie County had established a public trust in 1990 to receive these monies, its principal today would exceed $1 million.

In any endeavor in which our noble aspirations exceeded our financial abilities, the trust could fill in. We might supplement winter heating assistance if federal funds dry up, improve public waterfront space near the popular Hatch Restaurant, or purchase a much needed air conditioning system for Old County Hall.

Certainly, there will be voices explaining why we can't do this. I prefer to concentrate on how we can. Toward that end, and as a starting point, I've forwarded a proposed bill to those Albany legislators with election law oversight responsibility.

Of equal certainty, this idea is not a silver bullet to slay all our fiscal problems. But perhaps it will be a small start, and as well create grudging respect for a campaign system fallen off the rails.

With growing public distrust over the tone and tenor of political campaigns, and the waste of considerable sums in conducting them, my idea may give rise to increased respect for those who seek office.

In giving a public purpose to political campaigns, this initiative may assure political benefit for those who run — honorable alike in what it gives and what it preserves. ❖

# MUST SEE T.V. ————————— October 1996

Along with the new fall shows, television is about to uncork another season of negative political advertising. The good news is that every candidate will have sufficient funds to produce these mean-spirited, manipulative attacks. The bad news is that some of that money is still in your pocket.

And the worst news is that we continue to tolerate a system of determining elections principally on which candidate can shake down the most cash with which to cloud up the most issues.

But one sole oasis in the desert of American political advertising looms on the mud-strewn horizon. The four commercial networks are considering providing free air time to the major presidential candidates for undiluted, forthright expression of their ideas and positions.

Under a plan offered by a coalition formed to improve political discourse, Bill Clinton and Bob Dole would take turns speaking on successive evenings beginning October 17 and continuing twelve weeknights thereafter. Their statements will address specific policy issues, take two minutes, and be given by the candidates themselves.

In addition, I think these addresses should be delivered live, take place at the same time each evening, and be carried by every network.

As a candidate for Congress two years ago, I had an idea. Rather than follow the tired practice of recording a 15-second spot and repeatedly airing it until viewers became ill, I decided to deliver all campaign commercials live. Utilizing technology that permits remote location broadcast, I spoke from various sites directly affected by the policies I wanted to discuss: from Seneca Vocational High School, I talked about the disparity in urban and suburban education funding; from Mercy Hospital's mammogram testing center, the imperative of cancer prevention and research; and from an East Side street corner where one Buffalo teen shot another, the horror of handgun violence.

My primary campaign was unsuccessful, but I felt the broadcasts my supporters and I put together breathed new life into the issues. Viewers let me know, in mail and comments, that they were grateful for our forthright approach. They said they retain more information than that imparted by recorded, slogan-based ads.

Pulling off the broadcasts — a complex matter involving transmitter trucks, satellites, endless cables, talented technicians, and patient studio producers — did not always go smoothly. Fever and flu kept me in bed until shortly before our health-care commercial, and I must have appeared rather green in the gill on the monitors. With 20 seconds to go to air time, I overheard one technician challenge a colleague, "five dollars says he hits the floor halfway through." It turned out to be one of our better efforts.

According to Charles Rand, curator of the University of Oklahoma Political Communication Center, that campaign was the first in history to deliver live broadcasts, address solely substantive matters, and refrain from personal attacks. Indeed, one broadcast in which I described my opponents' accomplishments elicited the most favorable response.

In our current political climate, even the most thoughtful of public servants will assert that negative advertising works. But they never pose the essential question: At what cost?

After several generations of ads concocted by the Dick Morris wannabes around the nation, we can now quantify the damage: erosion of faith in virtually every American institution; the skepticism bordering on cynicism with which young people view any public utterance; and an aversion to the brutality of politics that precludes accomplished women and men from serving.

The truth is that negative ads are designed in part to reduce voter turnout. They turn voters off so much that some never bother. Not voting, then, as Free Time for Straight Talk head Paul Taylor says, is to give cynical, poll-driven consultants exactly what they want.

President Theodore Roosevelt, who took the oath of office here in Buffalo 95 years ago last month, was once approached by a pollster with the latest take on the popular pulse. "I'm not interested in what the people think," he said pushing the handler away, "I'm interested in what they should think."

We should think that political campaigns serve purposes other than winning elections. We should believe that television airwaves serve functions other than to amuse or entertain.

And we should know that both politics and television provide opportunities to inform and unite us in our collective passion to improve our lives.

Virtuous citizenship — on the networks' part by providing the free time and on our part by viewing it — is not a cure-all. But candidates' forthright conversation of ideas and purpose, conducted over the powerful medium of television, offer our best hope of deliverance from the graceless age of politics in which we now live. ❖

# LET'S SEND POLITICAL ADS DOWN TOBACCO ROAD_____ April 1997

Washington promises to reform campaign finance laws were as plentiful as Buffalo lake-effect snowstorms this winter, and just as likely to disappear with the spring.

That is, until we disturbed Abraham Lincoln's richly-deserved slumber.

More damaging fundraising practices certainly exist: trading policy decisions for cash, or hawking bills written by affected businessmen.

But crowding America's affluent into the well-appointed Lincoln bedroom leaves the rest of us out in a log cabin, perhaps angry enough for the first time to demand change.

One insatiable craving has driven the Lincoln overnights, Vice President Al Gore's telephone pitches, Ohio Rep. John Boehner's distributing National Rifle Association checks on the House floor, and virtually every congressman's willingness to accept legal bribes from businesses over which they exercise regulatory control.

That is access to television's power to annihilate an opponent in 15 and 30 second bursts — at exorbitant cost.

Americans must now say what Shakespeare's Mercutio did before expiring in the feud between the Montegues and the Capulets: "A plague on both your houses."

The siren song of television advertising fills our public servants' heads, drowns out our voices, and lures them away from the cacophony of noises that comprise democratic process.

And because not one reform before Congress addresses this essential truth, as George Bailey said in Bedford Falls, we are looking at this thing all wrong.

Rather than regulate the supply side of campaign money — by further limiting amounts that candidates raise and spend — we should eliminate the cause of the unbridled demand for funds.

With 30-second attack ads bludgeoning our sense of public service almost as much as nicotine blackened our lungs, it's time to prohibit television political advertising by candidates for federal office.

The Federal Communications Act of 1934 — under which the American people grant licenses for the use of public airwaves for commercial purposes — permits us to proscribe certain advertising not in the public interest. Political ads fit that bill.

Both the content of political ads and the financing methods behind them demonstrate that they no longer deserve the privilege of appearing on the public airwaves.

Citing an estimate that paid political ads generated $1.8 billion last year, opponents will assert that this would deprive networks and their affiliates of considerable revenue. But this enormous amount was only 2.5 percent of television's astronomical ad revenue received during the 1996 election cycle.

Moreover, tucked into last year's Telecommunications Act was a gift to broadcasters of unprecedented generosity: For free, Congress handed over cyberspace, an immensely valuable area of public property, to private broadcasters. "Don't cry for me, Public Interest, the truth is I immediately left you," is now the digital-age broadcasters' signature tune.

But debate over that giveaway continues. And in light of recent disclosures, Congress should threaten imposing "digital spectrum" fees (just as we now exact payment for use of frequency "channels") unless networks meet expanded public interest obligations commensurate with their exploding growth. They should now provide free air time for candidates' policy statements.

Once we banish paid attacks and restrict television's role to free time for one or two minute issue discussions, we'll accomplish three goals: eliminating the endless need for money; elevating public discourse; and restoring confidence in our political process.

In 1859, supporters asked Abraham Lincoln permission to dress up his past a bit to enhance election prospects. Citing Gray's Elegy, Lincoln told them that his life story was "the short and simple annals of the poor." "That's my life," he said, "and that's all that you or anyone else can make of it."

In Delaware Park's Rose Garden sits sculptor Bryant Baker's recently restored bronze rendition of a young Lincoln.  Looking at it is a reminder that having America's affluent rewarded by an evening in his bedroom would have bemused and offended Lincoln's typically American sense of humility.

But if public uproar results in campaign reforms that restore faith in American political process, how fitting that over century after he led, Lincoln again pointed our way to a more perfect union. ❖

# A Buffalo Constitutional Convention_____September 1997

As debate over whether to convene a State Constitutional Convention becomes more intense this autumn, an intriguing pattern has emerged.

Despite an accumulation of state government weaknesses — from a broken budget process and omnipotent leaders to obstructive election laws and tyrannical incumbency — disparate groups have aligned in opposition to a convention.

Even those with persistent and now worsening distrust of government, among them the League of Women Voters, several environmental groups, and the Bar Association of the City of New York, are willing to forego a chance at reform.

Central to the thinking of convention opponents is a belief that any convention held in this age of special interest politics, money-driven policies, and closed door Albany practices, risks writing in regressive change that may make bad matters worse.

The irony that some who concede the need for constitutional change are willing to let barking dogs lie has perplexed those of us who view the November referendum as an opportunity to modernize and improve a worn document. Until, that is, you examine the State Capitol environment that gives rise to their concerns.

There is a safety valve: any new constitution would have to be approved by voters in a referendum before it could take effect. But the specter of a constitution being designed in Albany's dark corridors or behind its thick doors (viewing PBS' "Inside Albany" is like watching an American Movie Classics film noir festival) is still unsettling.

Indeed, the heart-of-darkness image that Albany evokes in truth reflects a harsh reality. Unlike the U.S. Congress, which underwent cleansing and progressive reforms after Watergate — reducing chairmen and party leaders' power, establishing meaningful committee systems, and strengthening joint conferences — Albany continues to operate with sensibilities and rules that would make Boss Tweed blush. And all the average legislator can do is lament, and accept, her or his lack of influence.

Combine that with a delegate selection process that is sure to make convention delegates out of these same legislators, and good government groups' reticence becomes understandable.

But there's a way out. To enhance prospects for true citizen participation, I propose that we pull the constitutional convention out of Albany and hold it in the City of Buffalo. Think of the advantages:

- Removing the proceedings from Albany would dull the edge held by lobbyists and special interests who know every inch of the Capitol corridors.

- Buffalo sits in the center of an up-state economy that is the sole exception to an economic resurgence sweeping the nation. Along with the "Thruway Cities" of Rochester and Syracuse, we are a fragile region in economic peril. And to the degree that constitutional regulations and policies impair our progress perhaps more than other portions of New York, it's appropriate that reform discussions take place here.

- Our State University of New York at Buffalo Law School (the largest in the SUNY system) and the University's new Institute of Local Governance and Regional Growth offer convention delegates legal and governance expertise unmatched in the state.

- History suggests that constitutional conventions last several months. Buffalo's proximity to the Chautauqua Institution — one of America's most historic centers for examination of public matters — may afford opportunity for delegates to conduct discussions and seminars to further enhance public participation.

- New York State's reputation as a creative center for progressive change can be restored by a precedent-setting effort to hold important proceedings outside the perceived remoteness of a stifling Capitol.

The State Constitution requires any convention to "convene" in Albany. It does not require them to remain there. So after a formal opening, delegates could recess, travel by bus through up-state communities — holding "town hall" meetings along the way — and re-convene in Buffalo. These town hall sessions would educate delegates in local and regional concerns, and strengthen their ability to identify appropriate constitutional changes.

Out of Albany, there's a better chance of producing a true peoples' convention.

To assert that our state system of governance is either too good to tamper with or impossible to change is wrong. And to permit distrust of the reform process to paralyze our will to try is unacceptable.

In an age where bold ideas and experimentation are advancing the reputations and fortunes of Wisconsin, Michigan, and Oregon, there is no reason why we cannot add New York to that list.

For historic, symbolic, and, most important, public interest reasons, if voters approve a state constitutional convention this November, let's hold it in Buffalo. ❖

# Peace Bridge
# Consensus Building————————August 1999

Several months ago, a series of meetings was held to examine Peace Bridge expansion. These design "charettes" included the Peace Bridge Authority, but did not invite all concerned citizens. A strong sense that sustainable agreement could not be achieved without inclusive discussion grew even stronger.

This month, we're having yet another go at creating community consensus through open, unfettered, debate. Funded by both taxpayer and philanthropic funds, the Public Consensus Review Committee has retained renowned consultants to assess all alternatives, and last week heard public comment for some twenty hours.

But an absent Bridge Authority did not hear a single word. Our progress has thus been from one process in which not everyone could participate, to another process in which not everyone would. At this rate of dysfunction, Hillary Clinton will soon be explaining that as four-year olds, we Western New Yorkers heard our grandmothers and mothers argue over bridges, and were thus forever scarred.

Of the reasons the authority offers for not participating, one is somewhat understandable. With litigation pending, and as the body with sole decision-making responsibility, lawyers advise the authority to remain mum. That counsel, accurately reflecting the authority's remote and unaccountable status under present law, is perhaps sophisticated, probably expensive, and certainly wrong.

For it leaves us with yet another process lacking integrity for want of inclusiveness. Worse still, it affirms the authority's decision to create public policy in confrontational court. Warring over a symbol of peace advances neither cooperative governance nor community renewal.

And heaven help us if, in this age of collaboration, the take-no-prisoners legal culture that produced both O.J.Simpson's trial and Bill Clinton's depo-

43
❖

sition drives our public interest. (You can almost hear an attorney explain, "it depends on what the meaning of the word plaza is").

Rather than demonize the Bridge Authority and curse their dark impulses, let's light yet another course by which authority members might endorse collaboration.

To their credit, the City of Buffalo, Buffalo Olmsted Parks Conservancy, and Episcopal Home waited until the last possible moment to file suit. The authority then responded with its own, and the battle was pitched. A respected commercial litigator estimates that with motions, argument, appeal, and re-appeal, resolving Peace Bridge lawsuits may take until 2002. Other social and economic challenges that require our attention cannot wait that long.

Commencing litigation has accomplished its original goal: to create time to craft an alternative design that will garner broad public support. With that now in progress, the imperative of PBA involvement outweighs the importance of spilling legal blood.

We who believe that our magnificent city and region deserve a soaring landmark bridge that conveys to posterity who we are and to what we aspire know that this conviction shall carry the day in any discussion. A free and open debate with the Authority, we fear not.

To create that debate, we must take one final, good faith step, and encourage all sides to suspend bridge-related litigation. Toward that end, I've prepared and sent a "standstill agreement" to each of the parties and challenged them to sign it.

Under this agreement, everyone preserves their right to future claims, but for now interrupts all legal maneuvers. It compels parties only to stand down, not give up — so should the need exist after a full and open process, everyone would be free to resume battle stations.

This agreement would create an unthreatening climate from which reasoned discourse can emerge, and may inject the PBA with sufficient courage to come into the light of day and defend their work.

If, as Louis Sullivan said, architecture is frozen music, than a bridge is a frozen embrace. With ancient, shapeless material, it expresses a timeless, human desire to reach out across generations, boundaries, and even the awesome power of nature. No building, convention center, sports arena, or any other man-made structure holds such transcendent importance.

And if ever a human endeavor merited caring and collaborative effort, free of the rancor that accompanies a lawsuit, it's our effort to build this bridge. ❖

# RACE

## *Race*

What happens to a dream deferred?

Does it dry up

Like a raisin in the sun?

Or fester like a sore

And then run? ❖

LANGSTON HUGHES

## EDITOR'S NOTE ❖

These articles addressing race in America the author wrote in response to specific challenges that the City of Buffalo faced during the last several years. The passage of time draws attention to the underlying reforms necessary to resolve social conflict.

# Race, Reform, and Regional Thinking; Lessons and Solutions for The New Century_____April 1999

In past weeks, Western New York became the vortex at which race, class, future hopes, and past failings met. Never have our abilities to speak with and learn from one another been more needed. And never have they been more absent.

On the Buffalo School Board, racial tension informed a question of competence; in the Common Council, a citizen panel retained Council size in order to sustain African-American voice; and in a criminal courtroom, an attorney charged the discreet racism of transportation policy with taking a young woman's life.

Against this backdrop, community leaders gathered in a University at Buffalo classroom. Under the auspices of a White House program, and in strained and at times angry manner, they discussed race and racism in Western New York.

Taken together, these events revealed that if men are from Mars and women from Venus, then our community's people of color and white people are from different galaxies. We're speaking different languages and talking through one another. And while some listen, too few hear.

Our inability to understand one another afflicts not only race discussions, but political, class, and public policy discourse as well. Western New York businessmen patronize elected officials; bridge builders assail community healers; and suburban residents lecture urban leaders. Like warring spouses in a dysfunctional marriage — shrieking at the top of our lungs — raw, distrustful words surround us.

How did we sink this low? At the end of the American Century of freedom triumphant over powerful walls, how can such petty barriers separate us? And as does the sensitive and forward thinking spouse, who among us will be first to summon the courage to say, "O.K., O.K., please, let's stop shouting?"

❖

# RACE CARDS AND EMPTY DECKS;
# THE SCHOOL SUPERINTENDENT INQUIRY

In the recent Buffalo School Board matter, one essential question remained unasked: What would impel a community leader to introduce race into a question of professional and fiscal responsibility? For as perplexing as it was to charge racism, our lack of curiosity into experiences and beliefs that gave rise to its insertion was equally unsettling.

We need only go back to O.J. Simpson's acquittal to find the prism through which African-Americans can see a fellow black man under siege. And it provides a starting point to understand how an inquiry into an administrator's competence can be viewed as an assault on an entire people.

Sitting among several African-American religious leaders last year, explaining my idea to get suburban congregations into Buffalo for inter-religious conversation with inner city residents, I claimed that Western New Yorkers were among the nation's most tolerant people. That was exactly the problem, a black woman replied. White people tolerate unequal economic and social growth patterns that have produced an isolated, impoverished, inner city surrounded by inaccessible, affluent, suburbs.

Perhaps this is the central truth to bear in mind. Yet again our nation enjoys sweeping economic resurgence, with growth permeating virtually every sector of the population except people of color. And for all the African-American communities in our city — as with white society, there exist several black communities with widely varying sensibilities — this is the harsh reality that binds them.

To this present state, add America's history of privileged whites profiting from assumptions of deserving the bank loan, apartment, and job, as well as the presumption of innocence. Viewing the School Board's inquiry in this context, the fate of Mississippi's James Meredith, Harper Lee's fictional character, Tom Robinson, and three young girls praying in a Selma church, quietly enter your consciousness.

The American minority experience is awash in endless denials of rights, and, indeed, life to those least able to defend themselves. Is charging racism, then, just another way of demanding fundamental protections, or maybe just an even break?

If it is, then we must find words more balanced and less divisive with which to make the point. For when any one of us cheapens the value of outrage — by cavalierly charging outrageous behavior — we undermine all those struggling to find the language of understanding and respect.

## GOVERNMENT CONSOLIDATION; AFFECTING POWER AND VOICE

Against this backdrop, reducing the number of Common Council members takes on another hue. We've learned how successful cities and regions throughout America are embracing reform to strengthen local government. But we've not learned the process and sequence with which to join them.

In recent years, but before we understood the benefits of reducing fragmented government, efforts to streamline functions in the suburban towns of Alden and Hamburg failed. As a result, City Charter reform effectively asked the urban minority community to be first in eliminating representatives — just years after their centuries-long struggle to affect public policy succeeded.

What if a predominately white, suburban government level was consolidated first? It would vest regional leaders with moral authority to ask equal sacrifice from urban residents who only too recently gained influence. From the black perspective, whites fled Buffalo — increasing both black population percentage and responsibility for the city's fate — and now ask minorities to reduce their voice. It makes no sense.

But it might if Buffalo legislative leaders collaborated with suburban town councils to set a timetable by which to downsize as a region. A regional framework would lift visions and views above narrow, district-by district analyses. And inclusive, county wide discussions would drive home the benefits of suburban reduction to urban residents, and vice versa, as well as affirm regional shared interests. In this spirit is found perhaps the most important aspect of regional thinking — one utilized from large cities like Greater Atlanta to comparably-sized regions anchored by Baltimore and Cleveland.

## THE ESSENTIAL ALLIANCE:
## CITY AND SUBURBAN GOVERNMENTS

Ever since the angry-white-male reared his ugly head in the 1994 elections, suburban elected officials have lacked enthusiasm for urban-oriented policies. As a result, Western New York's ever larger, sprawling domain has made us, somehow, a smaller people. In this failing, we are hardly alone.

But while we have just talked, other regions across America have reduced market pressures that produce sprawl, rewarded urban investment, and crafted development strategies that insure both urban and suburban futures.

They created consensus for reform by recognizing the global economy's newest truth — a strong, vibrant, character-rich city is a region's passkey to success. Nondescript, inter-changeable suburbs capture no one's imagination, and certainly are not what attract people to an area.

In addition, older, first-ring suburbs bear more resemblance to their urban core than to affluent outer-ring towns. Crumbling schools, abandoned residential and industrial sites, declining home values, and increasing crime pay no heed to political lines drawn over a century ago.

Why, then, should our public servants' horizons continue to be limited by artificial boundaries? They should not.

From Kentucky to Vermont, regions are creating more equitable ways to finance urban and suburban public education. Chattanooga, Tennessee rewards local transportation schemes that link inner-city workers with outer-suburbs jobs. And progressive states like Minnesota have adopted policies to accelerate minority housing in suburban enclaves. In each instance, both city and suburbs prosper as never before.

A long path beckons Western New York if we are to gain comparable success. But we are committed to the journey, and must now mature beyond old practices, still older prejudices, and embrace those innovations with which we can distinguish ourselves.

John Adams once wrote that while we cannot guarantee success, we can deserve it. And we deserve it not by squabbling, or talking at and through one another. We deserve success by transcending racial, class, and geographic lines that purport to divide and diminish us. With so many American regions acting as one, this is no time to permit history to pass us by.

## TELLING THE BUFFALO STORY

In "Gotham," a recently published history of the City of New York, vivid stories of difficult and virtually impossible moments abound. At every turn, it was citizens' emotional and at times almost pathological attachment to what the city was and aspired to be that saw it through. The "heart" that remains New York City's most recognizable trait, it turns out, dates back to its seventeenth century inception.

Like New York, we've encountered difficult times and prevailed over them. Through Depression, war, 1960's turbulence, 1970's loss of economic vitality, 1980's failure of the savings and loan industry, and today's population drain, we have survived and at times prospered. And if we are willing to sacrifice some individual interest to advance a collective good, our present challenges shall be no different.

But we can no longer permit fragmented community to hold us back. Cooperating as one, across old and tired boundaries, will prepare us for tomorrow's opportunities. For collaboration insures that every participant possess equal voice, which requires respect, which leads to understanding, which demands knowledge of each other's history and experience.

Taken together, ours is a unique story. It's a fragile, resilient, heroic, and ultimately triumphant story. It's the Buffalo story. And in joyous and healing language, we must now tell and re-tell it to ourselves, our children, our nation, and the world. ❖

# In Council Downsizing The Only 'R' Word Is Reform—— August 2002

Several years ago, in response to a dying city and dysfunctional region, Western New Yorkers of good faith and even better intention embarked on a journey.

Under the umbrella term, "regionalism," this movement seeks to address three aspects of our condition: political, economic, and spiritual. Its political aim is to increase government cooperation; its economic goal is regionwide prosperity born of renewed city investment; and its spiritual end is to remind all Buffalo Niagara citizens of their united interests and shared future.

In recent weeks, this passage to our future collided with racial echoes of our past, as people of color objected to the manner in which Buffalo's Common Council sought to reduce its membership. This accident could and should have been avoided. And if we're to reach our destination of a vibrant economy in a shared community, we must quickly repair the damage.

No doubt, the currency of charging racism to thwart change has been cheapened through overuse. But beyond the false shouts of politicians lay the true murmurs of those asking if a government that fails them now might soon forget them.

That won't happen if we hold firm to the central tenets of regional thinking. First, no area can survive — let alone flourish — today without a strong and successful urban core. That means those who inhabitant Buffalo's inner city — African-Americans, Hispanics, Latinos, and Vietnamese — must see their opportunities enhanced. And second, a united region that's growing is preferable to a fragmented community still shrinking.

Rather than fuel citizen concern about representation in a reformed Council, members should have described the benefits that improved governance can bestow: increased investment and jobs; additional basic and human services; and an urban government vested with the moral authority to compel more equitable suburban sharing.

By the same logic, a vote to downsize divided by race should have alarmed its proponents, and triggered insistence that their effort attract broader support. Reduction supporters didn't intend racial harm. But their intention doesn't diminish their perceived pernicious effect.

Blindly asserting that a united white coalition of Council members can effectively govern this city is only slightly dumber than contending that the status quo in city government is working. And both sides remain deaf to universal yearning for collaborative and not confrontational leadership.

In the end, neither race nor regionalism bears any relation to downsizing the Common Council. It is simply reform — necessary to place government in line with population change, and essential in restoring faith in a broken institution desperate for repair.

Throughout our nation's history, true reform poses the difficult question of whether government is a cross to bear, or an instrument of our salvation. It is neither, but it can be both.

And while our old job as citizens was to sit back and argue whose version of reform holds more truth — County Executive Joel Giambra's or Council President James Pitts' — our new task is to fuse Giambra's grasp of the importance of change with Pitts' knowledge that it can only be achieved through broad consensus.

The challenge of race has been and remains an essential chapter in the accumulated narrative of Buffalo. To meet it, we must understand that regionalism is a language, replete with a grammar of cooperation, syntax of sharing, and words and phrases of healing.

Council downsizing is too important a purpose not to proceed. But it's too important a mission to proceed along racial lines. And as we struggle mightily toward the ideal reform, we should together affirm its noble aim, and remain ever vigilant that it finds its mark. ❖

# REMEMBRANCES

## *Remembrances*

To be ignorant of the past is to ever remain a child. ❖

CICERO

Human history is in essence a history of ideas. ❖

H.G. WELLS

## EDITOR'S NOTE ❖

The author's strong sense of history weaves through all of his writings. In this chapter he presents several heroic figures, some with ties to Buffalo, many of national renown, but all leading lives of large purpose, fiercely devoted to community and nation.

# JEFFERSON AND ADAMS: "IS IT THE FOURTH?" AND "INDEPENDENCE FOREVER"_____ July 1996

Bright sunshine ushered Tuesday, July 4, 1826, into the United States eastern seaboard. No patriot could have imagined a more brilliant day on which to mark America's fiftieth anniversary of the Declaration of Independence.

While the infant nation had grown to adulthood — U.S. population had doubled from 3 to 6 million since 1776, with both New York and Philadelphia well on their way to becoming a metropolis — awe over the Founding Founders' achievement remained at teen-like adoration. The practice of reading the Declaration in its entirety at all Independence Day gatherings continued, on this day with particular pride and vigor.

In the Village of Buffalo— five years away from incorporating as a city, but exploding with activity — all 26 stores and 3 banks were closed as citizens gathered on the Upper Terrace. Westward travelers, merchants, and village residents made the area around the docks crowded, as had been the case seven months earlier when Gov. DeWitt Clinton opened the Erie Canal.

In New York City, Washington Square welcomed over 10,000 residents and visitors to an oxen barbecue spread over a table 500 feet long. During the program, the son of Robert Fulton accepted a gold medal in recognition of his late father's invention of the steamboat.

In Boston, the parade wound its way from Beacon Hill's State House to historic Old South Church, where a capacity crowd "squeezed to a hot jelly" threatened to collapse the gallery supports.

Over in nearby Cambridge, residents sat spellbound at an oration delivered by then congressman Edward Everett. Forty years later, he would deliver the principal address at the dedication of a cemetery at Gettysburg, followed by "brief remarks" by Abraham Lincoln. On this July morning, however, seventeen year old Abe was most likely devouring Weem's "Life of

60

Washington" or some other book when he was not working on his family's Indiana farm or earning extra money as a ferryboat operator.

But the two Americans who waited most eagerly for this anniversary's arrival, and for whom, perhaps, it held the most significance, were too frail to attend any formal celebration.

Fifty years earlier, John Adams and Thomas Jefferson had embraced the perilous American dawn. Since then, their own friendship had endured triumph, estrangement, and reconciliation. Now they were the sole surviving presidents who had signed the Declaration.

In Quincy, Massachusetts, Adams, 91, rose at his usual early hour and asked to be seated at his favorite reading chair. Having declined invitations from as far away as Philadelphia, New York, and Washington — where his son John Quincy was presiding over the official national observance as the nation's sixth president — he particularly regretted being unable to see even his hometown's offerings.

Atop Monticello in Virginia, Thomas Jefferson, 83, whom Adams once affectionately joked "was always but a boy to me," remained in bed after a fitful night. He, too, had declined invitations for reasons of health; he, too, had struggled mightily in hopes of seeing what he called "the Fourth." And, like Adams, by day's end he would be dead.

They first met in the second week of June, 1775. When Jefferson arrived in Philadelphia as Virginia's representative to the Second Continental Congress, skirmishes at both Lexington and Concord and Bunker Hill had already occurred. Assembled delegates were beginning to see a point of no return.

Adams, already familiar with what he called "the elegance of Jefferson's pen," soon succumbed to his serene personal magnetism as well. In a letter home to his wife Abigail, Adams wrote that Jefferson "soon seized upon my heart."

John Adams had to this point been the mind and spirit to whom the others turned. The most humanly engaging and, perhaps, brightest of the lot, Adams possessed attributes which today we characterize as "New

England Yankee" — formal, direct bordering on brusque, impatient, slightly intolerant of those less disciplined, fiercely independent, appalled at fawning, and in spite of himself somehow lovable.

Always short and then, at 41, already stooped and balding, Adams may have seemed like a curmudgeon, but his lightning wit and irreverent humor turned usually on himself. In later years, he wrote that as a public servant, "I sighed, sobbed, groaned, and sometimes screeched and screamed. And I must confess to my shame and sorrow, that I may have sometimes swore."

But the passionate Adams' overriding trait was a blinding intellect that rode rapidly ahead of accepted practices. His daughter-in-law once noted that "everything in his mind was rich, racy, and true." And as a raconteur, he was apparently without peer. He loved to tell about the night he and Benjamin Franklin, traveling through New Jersey in the fall of 1776 in a last-ditch effort to reason with Britain's Lord Howe, were forced to take quarters in a small room with a single bed. A two-hour debate ensued over whether the window would be open or closed. While Franklin marshaled scientific, philosophical, and patriotic sentiments in support of fresh air, Adams fell asleep.

But if you could not keep your ears off of John Adams, then you couldn't keep your eyes off of Thomas Jefferson.

Tall and sandy-haired in youth, he enchanted people with his placid temperament, kindness, and shy hint of vulnerability. In adulthood, his beam-like blue eyes, shock of red hair, and a face, as one senator noted, "always having a sunny aspect," captivated. He spoke in soft, low voice, saving fiery rhetoric for his pen.

Margaret Bayard Smith, a keen Washington observer of her time, wrote that when she first saw Jefferson, "with his face so benignant and intelligent, I felt my cheeks burn and heart throb, and not a word could I speak while he remained."

While the contrasts in this rather odd couple were evident, Jefferson and Adams shared certain qualities. Each man adored his family; both suffered unfathomable loss of loved ones, matters about which they could barely speak. And each harbored a distaste for all things English.

More important, they were achievers — energetic, disciplined, and questioning.

"May I blush whenever I suffer one hour to pass unimproved," a 20- year-old Adams wrote in his diary. Jefferson mastered the violin, mathematics, architecture, botany, art history — all without impairing his concentration on public service and the philosophy of government. He wrote several books and over 18,000 letters in his own hand.

Imperfections, of course, existed in each. Adams could be petty, complaining once that Jefferson "ran away with the stage effect...and all the glory" of the nation's birth. Jefferson would sink into depression if loved ones didn't respond to his letters, and only horseback riding or more writing would settle him. And, as with many public men, both could work themselves into a lather with some ease.

That Adams was blessed with a self-security sufficient to embrace the younger Jefferson's talents in the summer of 1776 dramatically affected the shape of history. He prevailed on the others to permit Jefferson to try his hand at the defining document, the Declaration, knowing that only inspiring and incendiary thought would move them.

As each signed his name to the completed document, they recognized the clarity, defiance, and originality of Jefferson's words as constituting their own death warrants. But sign they did.

"Sink or swim," Adams entered in his diary that evening, "live or die, survive or perish, I am with my country from this day on."

From that day on, Adams' and Jefferson's relationship underwent several incarnations. With the ascendancy of Washington to the presidency, jockeying took place among all those who wished to succeed him in office. Adams remained a loyal Federalist, served under Washington as Vice President for eight years, and then spent a single term as President.

Jefferson, sensing the Federalists lurching back to characteristics of monarchy, broke ranks. He opposed Adams for the presidency twice, losing in 1796 and finally prevailing in the bitterly contested election of 1800. During Jefferson's eight years in office and the four years that followed, they neither spoke nor wrote a word to one another. To an associate, Adams conceded that while they were friendly once, Jefferson had since "supported and salaried every villain he could find who had been an enemy to me."

But each began to soften by 1811, with Adams making the first move. When he mentioned to a mutual friend headed toward Monticello that he "had always loved Jefferson, and love him still," like a feuding spouse tired of the noise, Jefferson melted.

An increasingly affectionate correspondence ensued. If Jefferson wrote once, then two documents would post from Quincy to Monticello, with pleadings for more. Their remarkable conversation, over the miles and 14 years, is an eloquent and witty conversation between men of astonishing intellect, keen humor, and great affection.

"You and I ought not to die, before we have explained ourselves to each other," Adams once entreated. To which Jefferson replied, perhaps conveying more about the American paradox than that of two old friends, "And so we have gone on, and so we shall go on, puzzled and prospering beyond example in the history of man."

Jefferson kept up daily horseback riding until late winter of 1826, and Adams moved with ease and force until his 90th birthday. Without letting on to one another, however, both began to lose strength in early spring of the nation's 50th anniversary year.

In March, Jefferson, suffering from a painful intestinal disorder, composed a lengthy will. On warm days he seemed to feel better, but as it became apparent to both him and the household that he would not last the summer, Jefferson began to hold out hope to see one more July 4th. On June 29, a shaken visitor found him able to converse, but in weakened state. After the visit, Jefferson lapsed into sleep.

Late in the evening of July 3, Jefferson stirred and asked a granddaughter's husband watching over him, "Is it the Fourth?" When the reply, out of mercy, was yes, Jefferson appeared content.

He spent the night slipping in and out of a coma, at one point making the motions of writing, and attempting to speak on several occasions. Just after noon on the Fourth of July, his pulse ceased.

Up in Quincy, friends of Adams sensed that his powers of resilience were almost exhausted. He had taken to a cane and depended on relatives to read to him.

Sensing that he might be unable to attend even the town's Fourth of July dinner, an event organizer visited a slightly disoriented Adams on the last day of June. He asked for a toast that in Adams' absence might be presented on his behalf. Without hesitation, Adams responded, "Independence forever." When the visitor asked if he wished to add anything to such a brief sentiment, Adams snapped, "Not a word."

Adams lived long enough to greet the anniversary with an awareness that had escaped Jefferson. After an early rise, he requested that he be returned to his bed. Asked in mid-morning whether he knew what day it was, he replied, "Oh yes, the glorious Fourth of July," and soon lapsed into a coma.

About one in the afternoon, quite close to the moment Jefferson expired, Adams stirred. A servant standing alongside his bed heard him say, "Thomas Jefferson survives," the last intelligible words he uttered. After several hours of increasing weakness, not long before the sun set, John Adams was gone, too.

It came to be generally agreed that small, local services would provide the most appropriate forum for Americans to mourn the double loss of July 4, 1826. These services took place across the nation that autumn, including one at Buffalo's original cemetery on Franklin Street where Old County Hall sits today. Over the graves of Revolutionary soldiers who gave their lives for those inalienable rights to which Jefferson and Adams dedicated theirs, Western New Yorkers knelt in prayer.

They prayed that we the Americans of the future would exist; that we would know and understand the achievements of their departed heroes; and that we would celebrate the wonder that is America.

Is it the Fourth? Then, Thomas Jefferson lives. And independence forever. ❖

# MICHAEL COLLINS AND
# EAMON DE VALERA;
# VIOLENT CINEMA VERTE_____ December 1996

It's a long way from Tipperary to the Thruway Mall Cinema.

But through the magic of movies, legendary Irish rebel Michael Collins recently traveled over eighty years from County Cork to Cheektowaga where, in a dark dream, I witnessed Irish history as violence, and violence as creative passion.

History as entertainment is risky business. Even when the story is brilliantly conveyed, as it certainly is in the Hollywood movie, "Michael Collins."

But when the story line is Irish independence — a tale as old as America's 18th century origin, and as contemporary as today's tragic Balkan nationalism — an attempt to supplement the film's images with background and context seems appropriate.

"In the name of God and of the dead generations," began the 1916 Proclamation by which Ireland declared its independence. Little did the rebels know that generations of Irish violence and death were just beginning.

During the eighty years since the Easter Week 1916 uprising, historians have attempted to accurately place Ireland's fathers in the tradition of humankind's unyielding and at times violent lurch toward freedom. In perhaps its greatest feat, the film challenges us to comprehend what Collins and company achieved, if not reconcile it with how they achieved it.

As a college student, a twenty-something living in London, and now a middle-aged American sitting in a suburban movie theater, I've tried to grasp Irish history. While each attempt brings different meanings and offers different lessons, the haunting question of the morality of political violence is ever present.

In college, I learned of the Great Irish Rebellion of 1798, Ireland's most tragic and violent event prior to the 1840's famine. An abusive partnership of British viceroys and Irish Protestants governed the Catholic 18th century peasantry, whose poverty was unmatched throughout Europe. Fumes of the American and French revolutions settled over the island and fueled the thoughts of Irish intellectuals, including a rather sensitive, Protestant, lawyer named Wolfe Tone.

Tone's peasant revolt resulted in some 30,000 pitch fork-wielding Irish being gunned down. It also gave rise to the 1801 Act of Union with England and its exorbitant land taxes that would compel generations of Irish farmers to choose between starvation and eviction. A legacy of hatred and violence was born.

I learned as well of Daniel O'Connell, the 19th century Irish nationalist who devoted his life to repeal of the Union Act. O'Connell's Young Irelanders, deeply enmeshed in Gaelic history and culture, were determined to avoid British submergence of their heritage and faith.

Economic justice has long laid at the root of Ireland's sectarian differences. With Catholics unable to own land, hold certain jobs, have access to capital, or serve in Parliament, Catholic emancipation was paramount to O'Connell. After achieving it in 1829, his Repeal Association struggled mightily to restore Irish legislative independence. The group splintered over the use of force, with O'Connell opposing it, and the Great Famine's arrival brought the movement to an end.

Echoes of O'Connell's nationalism resounded in the Home Rule efforts of the late 19th century. Led by Charles Stewart Parnell, the movement for the first time urged civil disobedience. As an Irish member of British Parliament, Parnell utilized procedure to disrupt the body. In addition, he invented "boycotting" as a substitute for outrage by urging tenants to withhold rent from corrupt landlords, the worst being one Captain Boycott.

With this past as prologue, the Easter Uprising of 1916 appears a logical next step. In truth, the vast majority of the nation knew nothing of it and paid it at first little mind.

At midday, April 24, 1916, about 150 insurgents, wheeling an apple cart of decrepit German rifles, marched into Dublin's General Post Office and overwhelmed the few British guards. Outside, Padraiq Pearse, a writer who, along with fellow socialist James Connolly was intellectual architect of the revolt, read a Proclamation of Independence to a small, bemused crowd.

Facing the same odds as the 77 Americans at Concord when the shot heard around the world was fired, the Easter siege was over before it began. Irish women, angry with the urban destruction wrought by the rebels, brought tea to the English soldiers who marched captured Irishmen down O'Connell Street into Parnell Square.

Concerned principally with prosecuting war with Germany, Britain moved swiftly to end the insurgence. They immediately executed 16 leaders, including Connolly and Pearse. They had to tie the wounded Connolly upright to a chair to face the firing squad.

At once the Irish people were lifted, and the international community outraged.

Spared from execution was one of the rebel leaders, a quiet mathematics teacher named Eamon De Valera. Son of a Spanish artist and his stern Irish wife, De Valera's reverence for the Gaelic language had first brought him to the movement.

As he had been born in New York and could thus claim U. S. citizenship, Britain feared De Valera's execution would undermine efforts to convince America to enter the war against Germany. Ensuing years of political imprisonment and escape or release would forge a metal will in Ireland's future first president.

Spared as well, perhaps because his leadership qualities had yet to emerge, was Michael Collins.

Combining De Valera's devotion to Irish culture with a strong antipathy toward England's wartime conscription, Collins had quit his job in the London branch of Morgan Guaranty just prior to the uprising. At 26, he was a large, lithe figure and, as the film shows, one given to both angry outbursts and quiet gestures of kindness.

Perhaps lesser known was Collins' passion for things of the mind. Like De Valera, he was well read, possessed a sophisticated knowledge of republican government principles, and his letters celebrated both literature and the joys of theater. To this he added an infectious humor and an astonishingly cool head. At the height of the Post Office fighting, Collins approached his commander to ask if he could slip out for a date with a girl he "hated to disappoint."

In the tradition of the "reluctant hero" — at first hesitant to lead, but once engaged, ruthless — Collins took tactical control. Knowing the role the local police force played in sustaining British rule, he organized the Irish Volunteers (forerunner of the Irish Republican Army) into a lethal urban strike force. Both British regular troops and neighborhood cops came under deadly assault.

As a boy, he had read G.K. Chesterton's "The Man Who Was Thursday," in which an anarchist asserts, "if you don't seem to be hiding, nobody hunts you." Applying the axiom, Collins oversaw a reign of terror from the seat of a bicycle he pedaled through city streets dressed like a corporate executive in a three-piece suit.

With Dublin in disarray under Collins' havoc, and De Valera directing all Irish members of English Parliament to ignore that body and govern from Ireland, Britain opened negotiations that led to treaty in 1921.

A bitter civil war over ratifying the treaty broke out, with Collins in support of it, and De Valera opposed. In August of 1922, a sniper took Collins' life as he traveled to a settlement meeting. He was thirty-one years old.

Collins and his bicycle descended from Paul Revere and his horse, each doing his best to disrupt the aims of an occupying force. And the intense energy and charm he focused on anyone who might help the cause seemed not unlike the bold passion of Samuel Adams in 1770's Boston. Lurking outside of Harvard University halls, Adams would wait until the professor left, dart into the classroom and start preaching revolt. Many a Boston Tory were ambushed by angry young mobs after he finished.

De Valera and Collins would as well influence those that followed them along the path from revolutionary to statesman. In the 1930's, a young Menachem Begin cited Collins and his underground to explain several Jewish organizations' evolution from moral into militant forces.

But De Valera's methods of passive resistance and ignoring oppressors had an even wider and longer lasting effect.

Mao Tse Tung wrote of De Valera's moral strength in preserving Gaelic culture. Mohandis Gandhi spoke of Irish prisoner hunger strikes, acts that De Valera initiated anytime one of his own was mistreated. And during the 1980's Solidarity human rights struggle, Polish philosopher Adam Michnick described his resistance theories as derived from De Valera. Disregarding Communist censorship and death threats, he openly organized Solidarity meetings to discuss banned political topics. As De Valera exclaims to Collins in the film (a quote taken from a prison letter to his wife), "we shall beat the British by ignoring them."

As portrayed in the film as well, De Valera made several trips to America during Ireland's embryonic stages. His mission was always two-fold: to gain formal American recognition of the Republic, and to raise money. And his travels brought him to Buffalo at least twice.

Years before, after sending her young son back to Ireland, his mother left New York City and settled upstate in Rochester. As a result, De Valera's several visits to her brought him through Western New York.

In 1920, his train stopped briefly at our Central Terminal en route to Chicago, where De Valera pressed the Democratic Party convention to include Irish recognition in their platform.

And on Friday, April 1, 1927, after a day in Rochester, De Valera spent the early evening in Buffalo conferring with supportive Irish-American attorneys. The Republic was still not established, and legal ownership of the proceeds of Irish investment bonds, held in a New York bank, was in dispute. The New York State Supreme Court issued an adverse ruling, and De Valera sought counsel on proper appeals procedure from the Buffalo bar.

A balanced view of both De Valera and Collins is skewered by the prism of years of continued violence; a violence that De Valera detested and, had he lived, Collins would have abhorred.

The 1921 Treaty accepted partition of Northern Ireland's six counties from the new Irish state so that they'd remain under British rule. And from the

1948 establishment of the Irish Republic through present day, fierce and deadly debate over re-unification has continued.

But since birth of the Republic and institution of democratic self-government, Irish political violence lost any claim to the legitimacy of the oppressed. De Valera condemned the I.R.A. in 1926, and the Irish people outlawed the organization in 1936.

John Hume, principal spokesman for today's Catholic minority in the north, describes modern Irish violence as bearing resemblance to the American militia movement: contorting history in an attempt to rationalize criminal acts. He is right.

And yet, the unsettling question of the Irish founders' relationship to the legacy of violence remains.

Much more than with the printed word, human violence conveyed through movie images compels us to avert our eyes. And in our age of popular and perilous myth-making of Irish struggles, the sight of Michael Collins unleashing a violent, nationalist fervor that has yet to be turned off, deepens our understanding of the harsh reality of political rebellion.

Throughout human history, revolutionaries have been given to passion: sometimes inexplicable, often incomprehensible, but in their devotion to freedom, always inexorable. Through the awful grace of God, perhaps, they become able to accept the consequences. ❖

# The American President in Buffalo

For too many young Western New Yorkers, American presidents seem reachable only at the end of an uncomfortable bus ride, and history appears to happen somewhere else, but never here.

But to get a sense of presidential history on this patriotic weekend, it's not really necessary to bump elbows with the crowds in the District of Columbia. The spirits of several presidents can be found in our own Niagara Square, which possesses perhaps more presidential history than any other urban block outside of Washington and the other two early capitals, New York and Philadelphia.

Look and listen carefully on City Hall steps overlooking the Square, and you can feel Millard Fillmore's style, Abraham Lincoln's grace, Grover Cleveland's destiny, Theodore Roosevelt's energy, Franklin Roosevelt's strength, Harry Truman's art, and John Kennedy's resolve, all in the shadow of slain William McKinley's solemn echo of the world's most recognizable obelisk, the Washington Monument.

## FILLMORE AND CLEVELAND: NATIVE SONS

Buffalo sent two presidents to Washington, which is more than can be said for most American cities. Their statues stand in Niagara Square now, but they both tramped across it often in the flesh too.

Millard Fillmore began practicing law in the Village of East Aurora, where he lived on Shearer Street (now a National Historic Landmark) with his new bride.

After rising from the State Assembly to Congress to the White House upon Zachery Taylor's death, Fillmore retired to Buffalo in 1856. Along with his wealthy second wife, he purchased an enormous Gothic mansion on the site of today's Statler Towers. For almost 20 years, surrounded by countless portraits and busts of the former president, Fillmore held court there for guests from around the nation and world.

The death of Grover Cleveland's father in 1852 compelled him to move from Clinton, New York to Buffalo to work with his uncle. After drawing lots with two brothers to determine who would remain with their mother and who would fight in the Civil war, the lot fell to Grover and he became a clerk in law offices just off of Niagara Square.

Elected as both Erie County Sheriff and Buffalo Mayor, Cleveland occupied an office on the second floor of City and County Hall, now Old County Hall.

While Fillmore's journey from Western New York to White House took over twenty-five years, Cleveland rose from Buffalo Mayor (1881) to New York Governor (1883) to U.S. President (1884) in just three.

# LINCOLN: STROLLING THROUGH

After his plurality of less than 40% took the 1860 election, Abraham Lincoln wanted Americans to have a look at him. He insisted that his inaugural train follow a roundabout route from Springfield through the northeast to Washington.

Disembarking in Buffalo in February 1861, Lincoln told the enthusiastic gathering that he came so "that I may see you and that you may see me, and in the arrangement I have the best of the bargain." Excited fans dislocated an aide's shoulder in the rush to catch a glimpse.

The next day, ex-President Fillmore took Lincoln to the First Unitarian Church on Franklin Street, home today to Ticor Title Guarantee Company. After the service, they strolled back up Franklin to Court Street, turned left, and chatted for some time on a Niagara Square bench about local political matters and Lincoln's 1848 visit to Niagara Falls with his family.

History does not record whether Lincoln told Fillmore of 11-year old Grace

Bedell of Westfield. Stopping in the Chautauqua County town the previous day, Lincoln had called her to the podium and kissed her in appreciation of her campaign suggestion that he grow whiskers to fill out his thin face.

Five years later, Lincoln's funeral train passed through Buffalo. Many who had turned out to send him into office lined city and South Towns tracks to watch him pass into the ages.

## McKINLEY AND TR: GUNSHOTS AND HANDSHAKES

When an assassin turned William McKinley's visit to the Pan American Exposition into a nightmare, Buffalo did the best it could to save the president and deal with the embarrassment. McKinley lingered a few days and died at the Delaware Avenue home of John Milburne on the site of Canisius High School. Buffalo prepared to have the body lie in state at City and County Hall.

Over 150,000 mourners passed by McKinley's body in one day, the lines running up Franklin Street and filling Niagara Square.

Vice President Theodore Roosevelt, meanwhile, rushed to Buffalo from an Adirondack hiking trip and was sworn in at the home of his friend Ansley Wilcox. His diary entries at the time reflect immediate planning for his own administration. "It is a dreadful way to come into office," he wrote returning from City and County Hall to the Wilcox Mansion, "but it would be even more dreadful if I do not do all I can with it."

Roosevelt also showed a master politician's stamina as he personally greeted the McKinley mourners. Among them were 700 braves of the Indian Congress at the Exposition, led by chiefs Geronimo, Blue Horse, Flat Iron, and Red Shirt.

They all seemed to know Roosevelt, and shared an English visitor's observation that week: "The two astonishing things in America are Niagara Falls and Theodore Roosevelt: both great wonders of nature. Their common quality is a perpetual flow of torrential energy, a sense of motion even in stillness. Both are physically thrilling to be near."

## FDR: GREAT POLITICS

As New York governor, Franklin Roosevelt oversaw considerable numbers of public works projects, including Buffalo City Hall and the State Office Building, both dedicated in Niagara Square in 1930. As President, he saw our U.S. Courthouse erected across Court Street, and an additional floor added to Old County Hall.

His visit to lay the Niagara Square cornerstone of the State Office Building was marred by (go figure) simmering warfare between city and county workers. Tired of sharing the same space in City and County Hall, officials appealed to the governor, who led negotiations between the camps over who would use what in the building. State legislation memorialized the agreement until the new City Hall was ready for occupancy.

Who knows what Roosevelt's skills could accomplish for regional cooperation today?

Returning in 1936 as president, Roosevelt dedicated the federal building still used today as the U.S. Courthouse, an early initiative of the Works Progress Administration.

## HARRY TRUMAN: GREAT PIANO

Truman made a memorable visit to Niagara Square for a dinner in the Statler Hilton Hotel during his 1948 campaign. He arrived not long after a Newsweek magazine poll of 50 highly regarded political columnists, none of whom thought he would win.

It didn't look like a promising evening. Truman's campaign staff was dejected, local candidates were blue, and the evening dragged. Until Truman spoke.

He knocked the crowd out. And his energy and repeated insistence that he would prevail lifted the room to a pitch that those present would vividly recall almost 50 years later.

At 2:30 am, Truman was still playing the piano in the Statler's Grand Ballroom. The hotel front desk took several complaints from guests attempting to sleep.

## JFK: A SMALL DISTRACTION

On Sunday, October 14, 1962 President John Kennedy flew from Pittsburgh to Niagara Falls to support local candidates in the upcoming election. In damp weather, he climbed into an open car for the trip to Buffalo's Pulaski Day celebration in Niagara Square.

With a gubernatorial candidate and his local hosts sitting nearby, Kennedy delivered a strong if distracted address from a platform erected on the steps of City Hall.

Their plan was to motor back up to the Falls and return to Washington. But a flurry of activity on the south side of City Hall followed his speech as reporters were advised of a sudden change.

The president would now fly to New York and convene an unscheduled meeting with United Nations Ambassador Adlai Stevenson (pulled quickly from a friend's Hudson Valley home) on an undisclosed matter.

In a car racing back up Niagara Falls Boulevard, quiet conversation centered on the President's interest in how his hosts' children were doing. But other matters were also on his mind.

During the previous week, American spy planes had been photographing Cuba. Reports that the Soviet Union was landing nuclear weapons on the island were rampant, and Kennedy had sent U-2 planes to assure himself the rumors were wrong.

But as Kennedy addressed the Niagara Square throng, photography analysts in Washington were concluding that Russian missiles indeed sat in Cuban silos.

Historians differ on the extent of Kennedy's knowledge in Niagara Square that day. But those with him would recall his pensive but determined air as they headed for New York. Perhaps his first thought — prompting his desire to see Stevenson immediately — was to consider United Nations assistance.

Both president and nation would later learn that UN sanctions were not enough, and the missile crisis would come to test his and the nation's commitment to preserving humankind.

## ABOUT THE SQUARE

Inspired by Paris hubs from which streets radiate like spokes from a wheel, urban planner Joseph Ellicott laid out Niagara Square's design in 1803. Whether he envisioned it as a place where American presidents would live, labor, perform, ponder human extinction, and lay in state, is not known.

But that is the rich tradition with which the Square enters America's 222nd year.

In Shakespeare's Henry IV, Glendower asserts, "I can call spirits from the vasty deep." To which Hotspur replies, "Why so can I, or so can any man, but will they come when you call for them?"

This Independence Day weekend, Niagara Square might be a good place to try. ❖

# SAINT PATRICK'S LIFELONG MARCH FOR HUMANITY———— March 2000

With each step that today's Saint Patrick's Day parade marchers take, they unwittingly echo the young Patrick's own long walk to freedom.

Abducted from his home in Roman Britain in the year 401, and sold into Irish warlord slavery, Patricius (as he called himself) herded sheep for most of his teenage years. His master, he later remembered, denied him clothing, shelter, and human contact, making hunger and coldness his only companions. And in Ireland's darkest of ages — "here be monsters" is how medieval maps described the island — making it through the night was never certain.

As with some before and countless others after, dire straits turned young Patricius to prayer. Writing in his "Confession" years later, he recalled saying "hundreds and hundreds of prayers" each day to forget the cold and allay his fear. Before his kidnapping, as a Briton teen looking forward to middle class comforts, he remembered thinking of faith as pure folly.

After six years in slavery, Patrick heard a voice say, "Your hungers are rewarded. You are going home. Your ship is ready." The only problem was his inland isolation was some two hundred miles from seashore. Setting out on foot, in constant danger from roving tribes, the now hardened twenty-something walked to what is today the Wexford coast. From there he sailed home.

Then came Patrick's saintly decision. Hearing yet another inner voice, he decided to become a Catholic priest and return to the very same Irish people who had enslaved him. In so doing, Patrick became the first missionary bishop in history, as well as the first missionary to barbarians beyond the reach of Roman law. His parents were, to say the least, mortified.

In the thirty years he spent in Ireland, Patrick offered its warrior culture faithful alternatives to pagan practices. That he physically survived is testament to his bravery; that he mentally survived reflects a temperament and humor that was, well, Irish.

By meeting the Irish people's highest standard — that of personal courage — Patrick won acceptance. He refused to fear the Irish, and they loved him for it. And by all historical accounts, his personality meshed with theirs: confident, earthy, warm, never taking himself too seriously, and able to find lightness in even the darkest moments.

But he possessed as well a blazing temper, and one that flared most against inhumane treatment of others. His teachings ended human sacrifice in Ireland, and greatly reduced inter-tribal warfare. And he was fiercely protective of those most vulnerable, particularly women.

In a politically astute letter to English bishops, he once railed against a king who kidnapped Irish women and brought them to England for slavery, murder, or worse. "It is not right to pay court to such men nor take food and drink in their company," he wrote, pressing for the murderer king's excommunication from the church. Statements like these saved countless Irish lives.

Patrick's assertion that one could "expect to be murdered or enslaved every day and yet be a person without sword or desire to harm" was somehow lost on the Irish over the centuries. It's painful to think what his reaction would be to Ireland's sad centuries of political and religious warfare.

And yet he remains a powerful voice. Indeed, the first human voice raised against slavery and violence, with a zeal fully comprehended perhaps only by those who shared comparable experiences of imprisonment, like Ireland's Eamon de Valera, India's Mahatma Gandhi, or South Africa's Nelson Mandela.

"I come in God's strength," was Patrick's greeting, "and have nothing to fear." It's a sentiment given physical expression today by American marchers here in Buffalo and across the nation. ❖

# Tonight's Presidential Debate Takes Us Face To Face With History_____ October 2000

How many evenings can you turn on the television and connect yourself to Abraham Lincoln, John Kennedy, and Ronald Reagan. Tonight you can. Tonight you should.

In our nation's history, only six previous presidential campaigns have seen candidates for America's highest office face each other and the nation. When Al Gore and George W. Bush walk onto the stage in Boston this evening, they shall step into that history. We owe it to ourselves and our nation's future to watch and listen as they do.

The brainchild of a network president, the advent of televised debates followed fairly quickly on the heels of the tube's 1946 American adoption. Harry Truman's acceptance speech at the 1948 Democratic Convention was T.V.'s first foray into national politics, and the 1952 conventions were the first covered by "anchors" and correspondents.

By 1960, two considerations converged to produce the first presidential debates. The medium's abilities and viewers had become sophisticated and large enough to warrant collaboration with the political process. And the cost of television advertising already neared prohibitive levels for the John Kennedy — Richard Nixon contest of that year.

In response, every American television and radio network offered the two major candidates free time for "joint discussions" on the condition that Congress suspend its rule that required equal time for fringe candidates. In perhaps its most important action of that session, Congress agreed, and the "Great Debates of 1960" were on. Almost.

Just as Gore and Bush did this autumn, Kennedy and Nixon approached debate negotiations with caution. The networks proposed eight evenings in all, including four in which the candidates would quiz each other without any questioners. They eventually settled on four encounters — with journalists, specific topics, free wheeling discussion, and eight-minute opening statements (this was long before MTV reduced our attention span to coincide with the length of pop songs).

And for the first time since Lincoln faced Stephen Douglas in seven senate debates, large numbers of Americans witnessed their public servants in open discussion. Ten thousand people turned out for the first Lincoln-Douglas meeting in Ottawa, Illinois. One hundred years later, seventy million Americans saw Kennedy and Nixon face each other about sixty miles up the Illinois River in Chicago.

In his opening sentence, Kennedy quoted Lincoln's 1860 question to Douglas, "whether this nation can exist half free and half slave," and analogized it to a then present communist threat. In so doing, he traversed the century that separated the two debates and connected himself and his policies to one of America's premier historic figures. In many ways, Nixon never recovered.

Leaving the stage, Kennedy was engulfed by a band of advisors, among them my father. Like their candidate, they were all young in age and veterans of world war, who spoke the irreverent vernacular that war produced. With broad smiles and not a few whoops, they pronounced Kennedy as having kicked, shall we say, the stuffing out of his opponent. "No gloating," he quietly replied. And after calling his father from a pay telephone, Kennedy turned to them, said simply, "let's get out of here," and disappeared into the night.

For legal and political reasons, presidential debates disappeared for sixteen years after that evening, until being restored in 1976. In subsequent encounters, Ronald Reagan conveyed his charm, Gerald Ford revealed his absence of mind, and George Bush Sr. became bored and looked at his watch. Each of their election fortunes was profoundly influenced by their debate performance. And the same will be true tonight.

As with many uniquely American practices, these debates are fragile gifts, and ones that can disappear anytime. So remind a friend, and be sure to tell a young person. Tonight, together, America makes history yet again. ❖

# FATHER BAKER: ON BUFFALO'S
# BEST BEHAVIOR————————————— August 2001

"Through our great good fortune," Oliver Wendell Holmes wrote about growing up during the Civil War, "in our youth our hearts were touched with fire." And among his generation that came of age during the 1860's, forever changed by the inhumanity of war, was a gentle, wiry teenager from Buffalo named Nelson Henry Baker.

When we think of what constitutes a full, meaningful, and constructive life, we ponder those traits that inform strong character. What experiences develop such attributes, we wonder, and how are those traits discovered and sustained.

In this light, Monsignor Nelson Baker comes to mind with increasing frequency. Perhaps not only because of America's renewed spiritual awareness, but also due to the large purpose to which Father Baker committed his life, and the integrity and grace with which he lived it.

Devoting yourself to impoverished children in a working class town, before formal adoption was the norm and when abandoned children were everywhere, is certainly among the noblest of pursuits. And establishing a renowned religious center in which to serve them — built and paid for by average Americans throughout the nation — is nothing short of heroic. Nelson Baker did both, with stunning originality and unparalleled success.

So from where did his sheer goodness originate? And how did he accomplish such singular achievements?

By all accounts, Nelson's first twenty years gave little suggestion of the life of religious service he would assume. He was born in 1841 at the corner of Oak and Huron streets on Buffalo's lower East Side, and raised behind the family grocery store on Batavia Street, now Broadway.

Bright, aware, mischievous — as a teenage prank, he once switched the outdoor signs of the Democratic and Republican party headquarters — Nelson could play a mean guitar, and wasn't shy about belting out a favorite song.

Lean and slight of frame, he walked quickly, thought even quicker, was something of an athlete, and enjoyed a lifetime love of baseball. His three brothers considered him stoic, understated, and of wise counsel. In short, Nelson was alive and aware.

My mother, who as a grammar school student at Our Lady of Victory received her year-end report card from Father Baker, recalls him in his final years as having watery blue eyes, framed by a soft and placid face.

But as a young man, he was fiercely willed, with even fiercer self-discipline. A review of the diary he kept reveals frequent self-testing, mental and physical, for no other reason than to strengthen his spirit. His life-long ability to kneel in prayer for hours on end — even into his nineties — can be traced to an adolescent habit of testing his endurance. And this self-discipline contributed to one of his life-shaping experiences.

As historian Shelby Foote has written, the Civil War was America's crossroads, with the 3-day encounter of northern and southern troops in the rolling hills of Gettysburg, its turning point. And as a Union Army private, young Baker witnessed that horrific battle's waning hours.

When Confederate General Robert E. Lee invaded Pennsylvania in June 1863, rumors quickly spread throughout Buffalo that the rebels were headed this way. As a result, New York State ordered the induction of 20,000 additional troops, and recruiting tents sprung up throughout Western New York.

Baker was delivering groceries for his father when he heard of the need for more volunteers. And on June 18, 1863, as General Lee was crossing into Maryland and heading north, 21 year-old Nelson signed on as a private with the 74th New York State Regiment of Militia. That night, he was shipped by train to Harrisburg, Pennsylvania.

The Battle of Gettysburg arose from a chance encounter. One of General Lee's brigades, sent into the town to find fresh stocks of shoes, found instead a small number of Union troops. On his own initiative, the young Confederate in charge of the brigade advanced toward Gettysburg just as an enormous Union corps arrived.

Some of humankind's fiercest fighting ensued, replete with violent cavalry thrusts and the terror of hand to hand combat. Over three July days, at one place, 51,000 men were lost, virtually equaling the number of Americans taken in the entire Viet Nam conflict. By the morning of July 5, 1863 Lee's army was in full retreat.

That Fourth of July, Nelson Baker was officially sworn into service in Mount Union, Pennsylvania, between Harrisburg and Gettysburg. Since arriving there in late June, he'd performed scouting duties for his company, and demonstrated both athletic ability and willingness to volunteer for hazardous nighttime duty.

Early on the morning of July 5, Baker's regiment was ordered to march into Maryland. Lee's army was retreating, and the Union quickly marshaled all available troops to give chase. The march was a brutal one in heavy rains, and the region was filled with wounded and disoriented Confederate soldiers, separated from their ranks and considered dangerous.

One evening on night watch, Private Baker stumbled upon a young Confederate private, seriously wounded and unconscious. Baker revived the soldier and carried him on his back to his Union camp.

A few days later, the New York regiment slipped into Clear Spring, Maryland, near the Potomac River. They camped near a mountain base, and that night Private Baker was ordered to lead a contingent of scouts to find Lee's position. He climbed the mountainside along with a handful of men, and in the moonlight shimmied up a tree to view the opposite ravine. Within a mile lay some 15,000 of Lee's troops, quietly crossing the river. The New Yorkers numbered just over a thousand.

Armed with Private Baker's intelligence, the commander knew the regiment was in danger. He instructed several companies to guard against night attack, ordered the balance of the Regiment to absolute silence, and hoped the Confederates wouldn't find their outnumbered Union counterparts. Relief arrived some days later, by which time Lee had successfully crossed the entire Army of the South safely back onto Confederate soil. But not before Nelson Baker had seen human suffering first-hand and up close.

In the wake of war, Nelson shared his generation's impulse to question life's purpose. He began his own feed and flour business, which prospered, and wondered where he would ultimately fit in. Perhaps his mother's faith, combined with his generous nature, led him to a Catholic seminary in Niagara Falls, where he began studying for the priesthood.

But as with other imperfect men who adversity shaped into greatness — a self-absorbed Franklin Roosevelt transformed by polio into an empathetic spirit; or a grief stricken Thomas Jefferson vowing not to waste a single moment of life after losing his young wife — yet another challenge would temper Baker's character.

At seminary, Nelson contracted a blood disorder which sapped his seemingly endless energy and led to his receiving the church's sacrament of last rites four times before age 40. Life for him suddenly became precious. And using it to reduce the suffering of others, imperative.

Such was the nature and experience of the young priest who arrived in 1882 at Limestone Hill (now Lackawanna) to oversee Saint Patrick's Church and its two small buildings — an orphanage and an institution for boys. Over the next forty years, Father Baker would build a complex of homes and institutions that cared for infants, young children, and adolescents from around America.

He financed his work principally through direct mail solicitation, a practice he all but invented when he realized that local parishioners couldn't possibly support the care he intended to provide. He wrote to postmasters around the country, asking for the names of local Catholic women. Knowing they would understand his mission to serve children, he formed the Association of Our Lady of Victory and began soliciting gifts. For several generations, Americans responded. And with their help, Baker made his vision reality.

Moved by a newspaper account of the remains of abandoned children found where the Erie Canal met the Buffalo River, Baker established his Infant Home in 1907. Its most well known fixture was a small bassinet, complete with pillow and blankets, which stood just inside the Home's entrance. Any distressed mother could at any time leave her baby in the bassinet, with no questions asked. And any abandoned baby would be quickly cared for.

Critics asserted that Baker was "condoning sin," making it too easy for unwed mothers. He paid them no mind. He refused to divulge names of women who utilized his services to government regulators, wouldn't permit any criticism of them, and seemed "structurally incapable," as one assistant remembered, of focusing on anything but the babies.

Next, he constructed Our Lady of Victory Hospital, completed in 1919.

Intended originally for the privacy and special care of unwed mothers, Baker succumbed to pressure to expand it into a general hospital only as a way to get registered nurses to train there.

Around this time, workers at the Lackawanna Steel Corporation went on strike over poor working conditions. The company's response was to lock the men out of their company-owned homes, many with families and children. For the duration of the dispute, Baker housed hundreds of workers, and in the face of company threats, fed and clothed them. As a result, for several generations, the mere mention of Father Baker's name in any steel mill in America evoked wild cheers.

Finally, in 1921, at age 78, Father Baker began construction of a shrine to Our Lady of Victory. As a young man, he'd traveled to Rome to see Pope Pius IX. En route, he stopped in France and was touched by stories of healing that allegedly took place at Our Lady of Victory Church in Paris. It was then that he decided to devote his spiritual life to the mother of Jesus under her "Lady of Victory" name.

But perhaps Baker's most compassionate work came during the years of the Great Depression. While others turned away, he refused to deny anyone in need. And it was during those years that he placed Western New York in the world's imagination as a center of caring.

After his death in 1936 at age 94, it was commonplace for exasperated parents to warn their children to "behave, or we'll take you to Father Baker's." But their admonitions missed the point of Baker's life, and skewered the uniqueness of his gifts.

For over sixty years, for countless abandoned infants, unloved children, or wayward adolescents, it was the fortunate ones who ended up in Father Baker's tender care. As for the rest, there's little doubt that he endlessly sought to reach them as well.

Late in his tenure as head of Our Lady of Victory Homes, a delegation of lay leaders approached a now feeble and failing Baker. They'd become increasingly concerned with his practice of holding regular sessions in which impoverished Western New Yorkers lined up to see him, and he dispensed money and other items belonging to the parish. Delicately, they suggested that while certainly well intentioned, perhaps he was "giving too much."

Father Baker thought for some moments, and then sat silent. Finally, he replied that when his time came, and he had to account for himself to some divine entity, "I'm not certain whether he'll ask if I gave too much. But I'm absolutely sure that he'll ask if I gave." ❖

# THEODORE ROOSEVELT IN BUFFALO

*The Special Relationship Between America's Greatest City*
*and Personality of Their Time* ————————————— **September 2001**

**W**ith the press of people filling its small atrium, it was becoming hot in Buffalo's County and City Hall. The September day was mild, but the air was heavy and solemn as the body of the slain President of the United States, William McKinley, lay in state.

Western New Yorkers and visitors from around the world who were in Buffalo for the Pan American Exposition had begun filing past the casket some five hours ago. The line stretched out the door and up Franklin Street all the way to North. And as the afternoon waned, perspiration and sadness weighed heavy on mourners as they paid silent respect to McKinley before a funeral train bore him home to Canton, Ohio.

The nation's new president, Theodore Roosevelt, stood near the casket on the north side of the lobby. After several hours of shaking every visitor's hand, he was the picture of life. In stark relief to the darkness permeating the building, if not the entire nation, Roosevelt's mere presence seemed to lift every downcast face as it turned from the sad casket to catch a glimpse of him.

After meeting TR that Sunday, September 15, 1901, an English tourist wrote home, "there are two natural wonders in America: Niagara Falls and Theodore Roosevelt. They're both loud, always moving, and thrilling to be near." By the end of his seven years as president, it was an assessment that would be shared by people throughout the world.

With the nation yearning for authentic leadership, the centennial of Theodore Roosevelt's presidency could not have arrived at a better time. For any examination of Roosevelt reveals that at one time, American presidents really did evoke fervor and swell pride. And the national symposium on his presidency, to be held September 14th and 15th at Canisius College, may suggest that perhaps one day, they will again.

As he stood one hundred years ago in the candle and incandescent light of what is today Old County Hall, Theodore Roosevelt's mind, as usual, moved quickly. His diary entries that evening reveal his revulsion at the assassin's act, concern for the nation's future, and most vividly, the beginnings of ideas that would shape his administration, re-invigorate the presidency, and set the nation off on the America Century.

And it all began right here in Buffalo, which in the autumn of 1901 was among the world's fastest growing cities.

But this was hardly TR's first Western New York visit. Indeed, he seemed to cross paths with Buffalo at seminal moments in his personal and professional life. Second only to his New York City birthplace and Long Island home, Buffalo held for Roosevelt more memories and evoked more complex emotions than any other city he knew.

And in the few quiet moments he had that September afternoon — riding in his carriage down Delaware Avenue with his friend, Ansley Wilcox; moving past the Niagara Square home of a predecessor, Millard Fillmore; passing the old law offices of his former New York rival, Grover Cleveland; and entering county hall and noticing the words of his hero, Abraham Lincoln, etched in the building's stone entrance — Roosevelt must have thought about all his previous experiences in Western New York.

The times he stopped in Buffalo travelling from Manhattan to the Badlands of South Dakota to escape the tragedy of losing his first wife. His visits as a New York assemblyman looking to change the face of state politics. And just weeks after returning from Cuba's San Juan Hill as a national hero, his first joyous campaign trip as a candidate for governor of New York.

Standing in county hall that afternoon, Roosevelt must have also thought how, after becoming president in Buffalo twenty-four hours earlier, the city would now hold a unique place in his imagination and heart.

"What a dreadful way to come into office," he later described his feelings as he entered the Wilcox residence, "but more dreadful to be morbid about it, and even worse if I didn't do everything I can now for my nation."

# THE ROOSEVELT ENERGY

Popular and respected author of 39 books, essayist published in virtually every American periodical, known as the "Albany Cyclone" from his days in the state assembly — as much for bounding up stairways as for legislative abilities — nationally-known reformer for besting Tammany Hall bosses, and Nobel Peace Prize winner, Theodore Roosevelt was uniquely American.

The torrential energy that was TR — "there seems, somehow, electricity about him," one commentator wrote — sprang from a sickly child not expected to see adolescence. Looking upon him as a white and fragile infant, an aunt compared him to a pale azalea.

Along with chronic nausea and fever, TR's childhood asthma defined the Roosevelt household. Rarely sleeping through the night, his father would hold "Teedie" upright in his arms so air could reach strangled lungs. And when he gasped for breath, Theodore Sr. bundled the boy into a horse-drawn carriage and drove him around New York's Central Park in desperate attempts to force air into his lungs.

Years later, of his heroic father, a large, gentle, man known as "Greatheart," Roosevelt wrote that "he gave me my most precious gift, he gave me air to breathe."

When he was 11, his father also gave young Roosevelt a challenge: to transform his weak body into hard casing for his already strong intellect. The young boy accepted, and devoted his life to fulfilling the pledge. The result was a life long obsession with outdoor exercise, nature, and hiking.

TR's "strenuous life" (the title of legendary ragtime composer Scott Joplin's tribute to him) rendered Roosevelt perpetually tan and seemingly lit from within. Neck bulging through his shirt and a chest widened by years of monotonous weight-lifting, his vitality caused something of a "tingle" in those he encountered — the word turns up repeatedly in written reactions to him. And what people experienced in his presence was a combustible mixture of mass, motion, and words.

After spending over four hours briefing Roosevelt in the White House on Middle Eastern affairs, an ambassador was asked what he was able to tell the president. "My name," he replied.

And adding to his allure was TR's love of life. "You must always remember," warned a friend who knew him well, "that the president is about six." And his kindred spirit with the unpredictable child within endeared him to friends and enraged his enemies. Hearing about Roosevelt's habit of making faces at passing schoolchildren on the streets of Washington, Mark Twain pronounced him insane.

"You don't smile with Mr. Roosevelt," a New York reporter wrote, "you shout with laughter with him, and then you shout again while he tries to cork up more laugh."

But this lover and producer of laughter was the product of unfathomable loss and pain. Not unlike the crucible of tragedy that tempered the character of other American giants — Thomas Jefferson's loss of his only wife; Abraham Lincoln's painful family relations; and Franklin Roosevelt awakening one morning to find himself crippled by polio — personal pain somehow transfigured Roosevelt.

Indeed, if life is not what happens to you, but how you react to what happens, then Roosevelt's story is one of unparalleled resilience.

## UNSPEAKABLE SORROW, 1884

Leaving Roosevelt's Albany apartment after a meeting in 1884, a New York Assembly colleague remarked, "he's a brilliant madman born a century too soon." Beginning his third term in the New York legislature that winter, TR was at 26 popular, successful, and on a fast track toward becoming Assembly Speaker. Politics was quickly proving his love.

But his other love, the one by which TR defined himself, was a petite and delicate girl from Massachusetts who he fell for as a student at Harvard College. By 1884, he and Alice Lee Roosevelt had been married three years, and that February she was pregnant with their first child. Roosevelt told pals he was hoping the baby would be born on Valentine's Day.

Standing on the Assembly floor on February 12th, an aide handed TR a telegram urgently summoning him home to New York. And when he raced through the front door of the Roosevelt townhouse the next morning, he found his 49 year-old mother battling typhoid fever on one floor, and his 22 year-old wife dying of Bright's disease on another. The next day, Valentine's Day, he lost them both.

Never again could Roosevelt bring himself to utter his first wife's name. At age 26, Theodore Roosevelt wrote, "my life has been lived out."

Inconsolable, he sought healing in the most desolate and distant portion of America imaginable, the Bad Lands of the Dakotas. Leaving the legislature and abandoning eastern life altogether, TR set off west by train. And during his many trips to and from a ranch he established in the Dakotas, he spent a good deal of time in Buffalo.

His letters to a sister during this period, written from the Iroquois Hotel in downtown Buffalo, make heart-wrenching reading. For several months, he could barely inquire about the infant daughter named for her mother, Alice, he'd left behind. And for his entire life, he avoided saying the girl's name, calling her instead "Baby."

Roosevelt wrote of the endless activities with which he busied himself out west — cattle-ranching, hunting, and any other pursuit that kept his mind off his depression. "Black care rarely sits behind a rider whose pace is fast enough," he wrote in his diary. Reading his thoughts from this period, over a hundred years later, his suffering remains palpable.

## A HOT CUBAN DAY, 1898

The still young man eventually returned to New York, served as police commissioner, ran unsuccessfully for mayor, and in 1896 accepted a position in the administration of William McKinley. But America's weakened military state at the time, along with Spanish colonial presence in Cuba, drove TR to distraction.

As Assistant Naval Secretary, Roosevelt did everything he could to provoke Spain and push McKinley into the Spanish-American War. It took him about a year. He then resigned his desk job and volunteered to fight.

When America learned that their Teddy was at age 39 going to Cuba himself, friends from his disparate and varied backgrounds descended on a Texas training camp to apply with him: Harvard polo players; upper East Side New York gentlemen; Boston Brahmin arm-chair athletes; and outlaw wranglers from the Badlands.

Together, they formed the U.S. First Volunteer Cavalry, immediately known as Roosevelt's Rough Riders. Over 1,000 men rode, lassoed, shot, and wrestled in the mud to be chosen, none with more enthusiasm than TR. When 590 were selected — among them seven from Western New York — many of those passed over wept openly.

Disembarking in Cuba in late June 1898, as the band they brought with them played "They'll Be A Hot Time in the Old Town Tonight," the troops caught their first glimpse of a small fortified ridge at the end of the Camino Real know as San Juan Hill. In the confusion and coral reefs coming ashore, Roosevelt lost one of his two horses and all his baggage. Had he not folded up one side of his wide-brimmed hat and sewn in an extra pair of glasses, he would have arrived for what he called his "crowded hour" all but blind.

In less than a week, it was apparent to the Americans that the Spanish had chosen two ridges overlooking Santiago — Kettle Hill and San Juan — from which to make their stand. Capturing each hilltop, fortified by shell launchers and troop concentrations, would all but take the island.

At daybreak on July 1, 1898, Roosevelt ordered his men to begin assault on Kettle Hill. By 9:30 am, in 100-degree heat, they'd advanced only a few hundred yards. Crawling through waist-high grass, a "steady, deathly streak" of Mauser rifle bullets tortured them for 90 minutes.

Having had his fill, Roosevelt stood, mounted his horse, shouted to his men, "are you afraid to stand up when I'm on horseback," and started forward. Steering less willing regiments out of the way, he rode over barbed wire fences and up the hill. A bullet smashed his left elbow as troops followed as best they could on foot. Within twenty minutes, Roosevelt reached the top of Kettle Hill literally alone. It took several minutes for his men to catch up.

When they did, they found Roosevelt's lungs heaving, his eyes alert, and as he later wrote, "the wolf rising in my heart." And as he looked across to the next ridge, he saw American troops meeting with less success. One must never shrink from what was "rough in life," he had written in his diary as a teenager, the same day he had underscored the Bible verse, "The wicked flee when no man pursueth; but the righteous are bold as a lion."

The Spanish were now fleeing to the top of San Juan Hill, and Theodore Roosevelt was in bold and hot pursuit.

He raced down the far side of Kettle and up San Juan, forgetting to order the Volunteers to follow. With Spanish snipers firing with full force, he roared back at his men, "What are you, cowards?"

Once again under heavy fire and up grassy slopes, cajoling and cursing, Roosevelt reached the top as enemy troops abandoned their position. It was about half way up San Juan Hill, one soldier later wrote, when "I realized that they would never kill him."

On Fourth of July morning, 1898, still holding the mud and blood that was San Juan Hill, Theodore Roosevelt led his troops in rather muffled patriotic songs.

Exactly eleven weeks later, as a candidate for New York governor, he sat in the Music Hall on Buffalo's east side, surrounded by company a bit friendlier than Spanish snipers.

## A WARM BUFFALO NIGHT, 1898

From the time he first learned how, Theodore Roosevelt ended each day of his life reading and writing. These seemed the only moments he sat still, and the sole time he permitted quiet reflection.

And on the evening of October 25, 1898, sitting alone in his Iroquois Hotel room in downtown Buffalo (the same hotel he stayed in during his dark trips to the Badlands) as he wrote his second wife Edith about black soot that splashed his face in Tonawanda that afternoon, he had much to ponder.

Quietly reading before an evening rally at the Music Hall, TR was 39 years old. In less than three weeks, his striking presence and vigor would help make him governor. And in less that three years, they would help carry him to Ansley Wilcox's Delaware Avenue living room to become president.

While New York's political bosses had acquiesced in his decision to run for governor so soon after San Juan Hill, they'd instructed him to stay home on Long Island while they tended to the campaign. But no one ever told Roosevelt what to do. And as it turned out, no one knew better what he should do.

That afternoon, seventy-five thousand Buffalonians had shouted "Teddy" as his carriage bore him along Chippewa Street to Main, up to Goodell, and over to Broadway. He never once stopped waving and shouting back at them. But it was all prelude to the memorable evening that followed.

At the Music Hall, an enormous oil portrait of now Colonel Roosevelt peered down on the frenzied crowd and official City of Buffalo welcoming committee. A troop of surviving Buffalo Civil War veterans, at TR's invitation, occupied the first several rows, and they hung a large balcony sign over the red, white, and blue bunting that read, "The Heroes of 1861 — 1865 Rally 'Round the Hero of San Juan Hill'."

Among those seated on stage awaiting TR's arrival were Jacob Schoellkopf, George Urban, Edward H. Butler, Sr., Frank Baird (who would later build the Peace Bridge), Chauncy Depew, Dr. Roswell Park, and every Western New York member of the Rough Riders but one, who had died of typhoid fever shortly after returning home from Cuba. They were all about to be treated to a four-hour political festival — designed and choreographed by TR himself — the likes of which Buffalo had never seen.

After an hour of prelude music, George Urban spoke for some fifty minutes. Chauncy Depew then delivered an introduction that warmed the crowd for the coming mayhem. The band played "Yankee Doodle" — driving the elder veterans all but over the edge — then broke into a wild rendition of

"There'll Be a Hot Time in the Old Town Tonight," the same tune with which the Rough Riders had pulled into Cuban port.

Suddenly, a Rough Rider trumpeter, dressed in full battle uniform, raced to the middle of the hall and blew the call to charge. From the back of the room, Roosevelt appeared, moved through the crowd yelping and slapping backs, and leaped onto the stage — all the while waving his now famous white Rough Rider hat.

The next morning's paper noted that at this point, the usually staid and dignified Schoellkopf was clapping and stomping his feet like a frenzied sports fan. And he didn't even like Roosevelt.

To ferocious applause and frequent laughter, TR spoke that night for over an hour. In his text is found several ideas that would later inform his presidency — outlawing big business' anti-competitive ways, protecting America's natural landscape from development, and supporting free people around the world.

By all accounts, of all the smiles throughout the hall that night, Roosevelt's was the widest. And the fever pitch could be heard all the way down to the waterfront.

Two autumns later, on September 14, 1901, and upon the death of President McKinley, Vice President Theodore Roosevelt returned yet again to Buffalo.

Leaping from his carriage, he ran up the slight incline of the Wilcox Mansion's front lawn on Delaware Avenue. Taking the steps, according to eyewitnesses, two at a time, he swept inside and ascended to the highest office in the land.

## POSTSCRIPT

Mid-way through the American Civil War, President Abraham Lincoln developed a policy of rewarding those cities that sent large numbers of young men to fight for the Union. He was particularly interested in hearing of those towns that sent and lost a number of sons disproportionate to their population.  In this regard, the City of Buffalo came to his attention.

As a result, it was decided that in recognition of Buffalo's contribution to the cause, the federal government would build at its own expense a harbor wall that Buffalo had for some time sought to develop and protect its port.

Construction began in 1868, and Lincoln's presidential commitment to our city survived his death and five successive administrations until the wall was finally completed in 1903.

When finished, Buffalo's break wall stood as the world's longest, spanning over two miles from Lackawanna to the Black Rock Channel.  Today, it's known for requiring minimum maintenance, and is considered among the best-built harbor walls in America.

In 1902, President Theodore Roosevelt signed the final executive request to Congress to fund the wall and fulfill Lincoln's promise to Buffalo.  When he did, Roosevelt took great pride in associating himself with an initiative begun by Lincoln, his hero, and even greater joy in giving something back to the city for which he felt so much. ❖

# RENEWAL

## *Renewal*

We differ from other states in that we regard the
individual who holds himself aloof from public affairs
as being useless.  But we yield to no one in our
independence of spirit and complete self-reliance. ❖

PERICLES

Ideals are like stars; you will not succeed in touching
them with your hands.  But like the seafaring man on
the desert of waters, you choose them as your guides,
and following them, you will reach your destiny. ❖

CARL SCHURZ

## EDITOR'S NOTE ❖

This chapter examines civic virtue and its relationship to our ability to consider important matters of the day — gun control, casino gaming, terrorists' destruction of the World Trade Center. The author asks whether we can find the courage necessary to achieve lasting resolution, offers proposed solutions, and challenges us to devise our own.

# A TIME TO HEAL:
# BANNING HANDGUNS NOW_____ January 1994

Today, 250 million Americans move among 210 million guns. Our nation possesses more handguns than children. And last month, some of each boarded a New York City train bound for the suburbs. Seven days after President Clinton signed the Brady Bill into law, on the Long Island Railroad 5:33 to Garden City sat an anguished man. After successfully passing a 15-day wait period and background check, he held a semi-automatic pistol.

Having bitten off his tongue, in the metaphor of writer Toni Morrison, and now speaking bullets to convey the language of speechlessness, he fired from side to side, pausing twice to re-load his multiple-round bullet magazine. All the while, the trains sealed doors held passengers at his absent mercy. During his second break, 3 men thrust their bodies across his, as 23 people lay wounded or dead.

Anyone who has ever feared the night was present on that Long Island train. Each of us who has either known or been touched by the horror of violence rode in that car. All of us who have viewed a T.V. image of a somehow vacant-looking mother weeping over her lost son sat in one of those seats.

And in the final analysis, every American was and is a passenger on that train, hurdling forward, confined in a country with seemingly no escape from the blood. An in the momentary silence of you reading these words, another gunman reloads.

In 1990, handguns killed 22 people in Great Britain, 13 in Sweden, 91 in Switzerland, 87 in Japan, 10 in Australia, 68 in Canada, and 10,567 in the United States.

Against this brutal backdrop, our children plan not their proms, but rather their funerals, telling friends and loved ones what dress they desire should a gunman lay them down.

There comes a time in each of our lives and, indeed, in the life of any democratic experiment in freedom, when we must examine our hearts, weigh those competing interests that impair our advance, and do that which ensures our continued existence. With the blood and watershed events on Long Island, the time has arrived to purge our freedom of the poison of handguns.

Throughout human history, when chronic violence reached unacceptable levels, the British ultimately spoke with Gandhi, Makarios, and now with the Irish Republican Army; South Africa spoke with Mandela; and yes, Rabin shook the hand of Arafat. And today in America, gun proponents and control advocates must shake hands with ourselves to bring the carnage to an end.

To begin, let's concede that those who interpret the Constitution's Second Amendment as absolute right to possess firearms are correct. As a consequence, limiting this property right cannot be accomplished without compensation.

In exchange, gun owners must acknowledge that their assertion that handgun control produces unilaterally armed criminals conceals a fallacy. At its inception, every gun is legal. They become illegal through theft or unlicensed transfer. To reduce the number of illegal guns, then, we must reduce the number that enter the stream of commerce.

And both sides must agree that today our public interest in eliminating the lethal combination of drugs and guns that has stolen our streets outweighs our interest in and right to private ownership of handguns.

Social and economic forces brought to bear on our cities have produced streets with allure far more powerful than anything else society offers to fatherless young men without education, training, or prospects for real jobs. Perhaps their daring reflects their desperation. In any event, until we provide equality of opportunity to every American, we possess a moral obligation to disarm them.

And I propose an initiative by which we might accommodate those who voluntarily forego certain rights so that this healing process may begin.

For a period of 10 years, I propose that we prohibit the manufacture, importation, distribution, and possession of any firearm able to be operated with one hand. The ban would apply to all guns and gun accessories whose principal use is crime — not law enforcement or sport — including military style, semi-automatic assault weapons, large capacity ammunition magazines that hold over 10 rounds, and low quality, easily concealed handguns known as Saturday Night Specials.

Prior to the law's effective date, Americans may either: a) rent their weapons to the federal government for an annual fee equal to the gun's market value (aggregate rental thus equaling 10 times market value), or b) sell it in exchange for the right to an annual federal tax break equal to 5 times the gun value for each of the succeeding 10 years.

Lost revenue resulting from the law will be more than compensated by saving taxpayers over $150 billion in annual expenditures to stitch up shooting victims and care for their families.

Penalty for violation of the law would be 3 years in jail. And upon the law's sunset, those who rented could collect their firearms, and legal sale and ownership of handguns would return in accordance with federal licensing procedures.

President Clinton contends that we are not yet at a point where Americans will support a ban on handguns. He is wrong.

While tragedies like the Long Island train engender temporary helplessness before our problems, our will is strong. We stand ready to embrace direction unfettered by political caution and unadulterated by the power of influence. We call it leadership.

And if we demonstrate a collective courage commensurate with the individual bravery of 3 Long Island men who risked themselves so that others might live, we will advance our nation into a new age of safety and peace. ❖

# WATERFRONT DREAMS AND
# CASINO NIGHTMARES——————— June 1995

The question for Buffalo is not whether we should permit a gaming casino in our city, but how in the world we arrived at the point of even considering such fool's gold.

The beginnings of an answer lie in the remarkable collection of revitalization plans that outlined ideas for our waterfront.

From 1948 through last year's creation of yet another city waterfront board, there's been no less than 8 city or county commissions, boards, and advisory groups. These bodies produced some 12 master plans, analyses, comprehensive strategies, and recommendations at a cost of several million dollars. None of these was formally adopted, yet alone adequately financed or fully realized.

Mayor Bernard Dowd's administration in the 1940's was the first to ponder waterfront development. A committee offered several proposals in anticipation of an era of declining steel dominance. Those ideas went nowhere, a fact memorialized in a photograph kept by former Rep. Henry Nowak in his Buffalo office. Taken at the time of the Dowd initiatives and now frayed and yellow, it bears remarkable resemblance to today's shoreline, absent the Tops' warehouse and Pier restaurant.

In 1971, Mayor Frank Sedita assembled a panel of entrepreneurs and, for the first time, paid consultants, to produce a rather ambitious "Buffalo Master Plan." After forecasting city population growth to 500,000 by 1990, and eradication of urban crime, the plan presented as its centerpiece the transformation of Main Street from Chippewa to North Division into an indoor mall. Elements of this idea were later incorporated into the walkways and tunnels of downtown Minneapolis.

Fourteen years later, Sedita-era optimism dashed by plant closings and brutal recessions, a new administration and new consultants introduced the 1985 report, "Buffalo Waterfront Project: Market Forecasts and Sensitivity

Analysis." It asserted that traditional Buffalo shipping activity would return to save the day. Unfortunately, the trucking industry had something to say about that.

For the waterfront, this Jimmy Griffin administration paper offered two solutions: an office/hotel complex called the "Pioneer Pyramid" and a "national focus theme attraction" highlighting Buffalo's industrial heritage with "low-profile steel amusement rides." An appropriate amount of dust accumulated on this document.

Fast on these heels came in 1986 a rather innovative idea to construct a series of canals at the foot of Main Street to echo Buffalo's ascendant turn-of-the-century days. Canal Place, as its author Ward Fuller called it, would be complemented by a Railway Museum and an oversized IMAX theater screen. While Fuller's pitch to Griffin was perhaps inartful (exclaiming that on the canals clowns could water ski on one ski), his innovation merited more than the mean-spirited slap with which Griffin killed it. Toronto's IMAX theater now attracts almost as many tourists as the one in Washington, DC.

With the 1990's came the city's Local Waterfront Revitalization Program (LWRP) and the county's Horizons Waterfront Commission. The LWRP offered the Southtowns Connector (with eventual Skyway dismantling) and a tunnel under the Buffalo River as two methods by which the waterfront might be opened.

Two significant considerations set Horizons' 1992 Action Plan apart from its predecessors. Rather than mere recommendations, Horizons' plan represents our first formally adopted commitment to long-range goals. It also includes an insight somehow absent from all previous work: that in order to attract commercial development and tax base-broadening residential activity, our region must first provide public amenities that enrich the quality of life. In our case, that means public access — visual, physical, and spiritual — to the water's edge. With all of Horizons' perceived deficiencies, chief among them its inability to gain authority to issue bonds to finance its plans, this simple acknowledgment represents considerable advance.

Against this historical backdrop (and several other proposals that met with similar fate — Marina Marketplace, the International Garden Festival,

Hank Nowak's aquarium, the Gateway Bridge), Mayor Masiello announces yet another waterfront planning group and expresses enthusiasm for a downtown casino.

Given the dismal state of city finances, the Mayor's surrender to the temptation of short-term, roulette-generated taxes is perhaps understandable. But we must stiffen his spine.

Gaming casinos register low on the economic development scale. They generate low-skill, low-wage jobs that trap employees in a hopeless future, add no infrastructure, and create an environment around which no family would live.

Moreover, one discerns a stalking stance in a company willing to self-finance an enterprise that depends on large numbers of people risking limited expendable income on a dream of instant wealth. While private investment is certainly essential, it shouldn't be accompanied by a predatory posture that belies our heritage of honest work, good neighbors, and kindred spirit.

And finally, if Buffalo blackjack replaces Buffalo blizzards in the nation's consciousness, we can say so long to Frank Lloyd Wright restoration, and perhaps to waterfront development that pays proper respect to our people.

I grew up on Lake Erie, swim in its waters, and seek out its shore in times of joy and challenge. For me, it possesses the beauty of the Hudson, the romance of the Seine, the charm of the Thames, and the historical significance of the Potomac. Our lake is the site of our community's birth, and that alone should temper our imperfect impulses and strengthen our resolve even in hard times.

Mayor Masiello must break the petty cycle of disregarding previous sound work. And we must fire our collective imagination to produce an original idea that will advance public interest and excite private investment. ❖

# Saving Private and Public Buffalo

When I could actually catch my breath during Steven Spielberg's "Saving Private Ryan," I wept.

Not just for those giant heroes, disguised as young American boys, who climbed out of boats off Omaha Beach and embarked on their journey into the ages. And not only for mothers who saw their sons disappear into Gold Stars placed in front-porch windows.

I also shed angry tears for we millions of "Private Ryans" whom they delivered from tyranny. In too many ways, we have yet to fulfill the gift of salvation with which they blessed us.

In the film's metaphor of life's journey, eight soldiers set out behind enemy lines to retrieve one boy, the sole survivor of four sons given over to God and country. "Can you explain," one searcher asks, "why eight of us should risk our necks for one guy?"

The two-hour meditation on the value of sacrifice that follows establishes the essential nature of giving to a full and meaningful life. As it turns out, before any of us can rest assured, reach shore, or return home, we must contribute, sacrifice, and perhaps perish so that others might live.

A startling simple affirmation of humanity, this. And one writ large in the story of our parents and grandparents, and their willing acceptance of families torn asunder for a nation strong together.

Only one soldier survives the successful search for Ryan. Having secured the boy's safety, the platoon captain lays dying. Drawing Ryan near, he whispers, "earn this."

Faceless then and forgotten now, if these fallen boys of World War II could be with us, would they say that we've earned their gift?

Sitting in the darkened theater, my mind's eye suddenly brought them among us. Freshly scrubbed and with youthful gait, they walk through my imagination, taking in an America struggling to restore a sense of shared community.

The boys seem pleased and proud of how we have made our nation a less hazardous and more civilized place in which to live. But what do they make of our social and economic landscape, where plenty and need sit as side by side as Orchard Park and Buffalo's lower West Side?

To fellows who turned Depression and World War into uniting experiences, I try to explain how we permit affluence and peace to separate us. I describe how the rewards of G. I. Bills, automobile mobility, racist lending policies, and a booming economy combined to create two Americas: one affluent, majority, and suburban; the other impoverished, minority, and urban.

They say not a word. But heads hung low, staring at thick boots, silently seem to ask if this is what they fought for. Pressing now, I note that free markets are harsh, some are left behind, and besides, isolated suburbia reflects a majority of peoples' desires. Their young faces go blank, until one pipes up, "Oh yeah? A majority of us wanted to go home after one day out."

Finally, they want to know what's on our minds as the new century nears. Over what do we argue, and of what do we dream? Not without difficulty, I tell them of failed bridges and intern's dresses, of powerballs and weakened workers, of local pettiness and a national void. In the youngest of the lot, the one with the brightest face, sadness appears.

As they turn to leave, I ask if any of them knew the Niland brothers of Tonawanda. Over his shoulder and with warm smile, one answers, "those guys are the best." With that they are gone.

Sacrificing individual interest for a collective good seems an idea slipping away with each passing obituary of a World War II veteran. But as sure as we must preserve their memory, we must sustain the values and ideals for which they fought.

In another century, in the face of horror of another war, Abraham Lincoln paid tribute to the "last full measure of devotion" bestowed by fallen soldiers on a grateful nation. A devotion that embraces both America and its underlying idea of shared past and interwoven future. That devotion survived civil war, informed the heroics of Normandy, and must drive our generation's search for our own Private Ryans — that is, those who could use a helping hand.

When Spielberg's eight Rangers finally find their boy, he and a handful of frightened Americans prepare to hold off what they know will be an overwhelming enemy attack. Young Ryan is told that he is his family's only surviving son of war, and to spare his mother further grief, his country wants him home. He refuses, asking only that they "tell my mother I'm staying here with the only brothers I have left."

As we prepare to create the world's first truly multi-cultural society, grateful for what we have been given, tempered by the knowledge of what finally awaits us, and inspired by those who have gone before, we must now express the same solidarity as young Private Ryan.

From Western New York's struggling rural environs to our most affluent suburbs, we must tell ourselves and our nation that we stand with our City of Buffalo brethren, the only brothers and sisters we have left. ❖

# At First Light:
# A New Century Beckons—— December 1999

We are all about to become old. No matter what age you are at this moment, in a matter of hours each and every one of us will become forever dated.

"At the end of the day," sing the impoverished masses in the musical version of Victor Hugo's Les Miserables, "you're another day older." But this New Year's Eve, the very second midnight passes, we shall instantly pass into a people from long ago, from that time before today, from yesterday. All of our stories, sensibilities, and experiences will come from the tired old man of the last century.

If we're not careful, the cherubic baby of the new age will have little interest in our deeds or dreams. And if we're not innovative and bold in everything we do, by the time it reaches middle age, the new century shall simply forget us.

Marjorie Baker Flickinger, wife of one of our region's pioneer entrepreneurs and a Buffalo social figure for much of this century, was born on December 21, 1899. She spent her entire life denying it, insisting that her birth date fell in 1900. She wanted no connection with yesterday, and for several reasons her sentiments were understandable.

Think of it: from the perspective of mid-twentieth century on, looking back on 1900 evokes sentiments of the old and out-dated. Those poor people of the early 1900's — God love them with their bone shaker bicycles and fragile automobiles — theirs was the time before America got going. They seem to have been born old.

Our practice of defining a century's start as a new beginning means that those living at century's inception are viewed as unsophisticated, and their work as preliminary. Along with unique privileges, then, to be alive as a new century and millennium dawn carries its own special challenges.

I first became aware of the idea of a new century in 1972. Having served in government for many years, my father worked with several Washington figures of the time. Accompanying him on a trip to the Capitol while a teenager, I heard former Vice President Hubert Humphrey say that he considered himself a "new century" man, and that he eagerly anticipated the new period.

Humphrey spoke animatedly to my father about the privilege of living at a time when an entire age is born and begins to define itself. He even had specific ideas about what public matters he would attempt to advance come 2000.

Along with countless other lovers of life we can summon to mind — some along in years, others shockingly young — Hubert Humphrey did not make it to this week. But we did. As a result, we bear special responsibility to inform our age with a quality of advance that befits a nation founded on the idea of endless experiment.

Our challenge is to have our innovations and reforms stand the test and scrutiny of the year 2029, or 2069, or even 2099. Our task is to act, think, and create in a manner that middle and late century Americans will admire and emulate; ideas, practices, or reforms that reflect awareness of the heightened duty that history has placed on our generation.

For us and our times, meeting this challenge rests more on improving community than advancing nation or state. A high bar, no doubt, but one that Western New York is poised to vault.

If turn-of-the-last century giants of government, education, and culture could be with us today, they'd be pleased with how we've made our nation a more civilized and less hazardous place. As well, they would be proud of the integrity and independence with which we have invested the individual spirit.

But they'd be perplexed and disappointed with the economic and social barriers that separate us within our own communities. For too many Americans isolated by impoverishment, it has been a strenuous life. And the degree to which American local government impedes efforts to create shared community, is the degree to which we have failed.

To meet our rendezvous with tomorrow, we must restructure local governance and redefine the notion of community. As we enter a post-suburban age, in which inner cities strive to regain economic investment and social vibrancy, the region has become the laboratory of democracy. And those cities that establish innovative relationships with their surrounding suburbs — across economic, racial, and geographic boundaries — will not only be tomorrow's successes, but as well produce tomorrow's national figures.

This essential alliance among urban and suburban governments holds endless potential. Across America, cities and regions are already adopting their own minimum wage, gun control, and education measures, functions previously considered the purview of state or federal government.

Their mission is more equitable sharing of resources and responsibilities across outdated boundaries, thereby redefining "neighborhood." Their purpose is to narrow an income gap produced by half a century of prosperity that has somehow widened it. And their aggregate achievement will be to draft a new bible for America's civic religion, one based on the ideal of the beloved community.

The next one hundred years will be a "Community Century," one in which the promise of humanity will redeemed one region at a time. The complexities of social, economic, and racial divisions will be distilled down, and thus revealed, to their essence: the moral imperative of caring for all we encounter and touch in our daily life. Only such a local covenant will deliver a national reality.

Beyond moral compassion lies an economic incentive for regional unity. With the end of Cold War and creation of the global market came realization that the most efficient operating unit in an e-world economy is the region.

Urban centers must be resuscitated, and social and cultural barriers dismantled, so towns no longer compete against towns, but collaborate together to take on competitors around the globe.

Throughout Buffalo Niagara, we've discussed these new doctrines. We've embraced change in our highest local public office. And we're willing to push our private institutions into new and more collaborative practices.

We possess not only manageable population size, but also a fiercely family-oriented people, willing to make life choices in the interest of posterity's children. It's difficult to imagine a region better positioned to both seize and benefit from the coming age, and in so doing distinguish itself.

In her public television documentary, "1900," Judith Crichton asserts that in many ways the twentieth century really began on an autumn evening in Buffalo. The horror of President William McKinley's death had brought the 1901 Pan American Exposition to a halt. For four days as the nation mourned, our city and its international guests were cast in darkness and silence.

Then, on the Exposition's final evening, its music once again sounded and its brilliant lights turned back on. Spectacular fireworks soared over Lake Erie, and with them the spirit of both Buffalo and America lifted as the energy and promise of the new day came into focus.

As it turned out, perhaps no other American city was treated less kind by the past century than Buffalo. But we made it. As Langston Hughes' character, Simple, once exclaimed, "I have been shot, stabbed, wounded, held down, shut in, locked out, underfed, underpaid, under-loved, and everything but undertaken. But I am still here."

Buffalo is still here. We survived accurate assassin bullets and misplaced universities, opening seaways and closing steel mills, and even "wide right" and "no goal." And we say let the new century begin right here, right now. Here in Western New York, where east coast sophistication meets mid-western charm; where our sense of place and identity is un-matched throughout America; and where we've waited some hundred years to begin anew.

"At the end of the day," the working poor of Les Miserables conclude, "there's a new day dawning." At first light, Western New York will be ready. ❖

# The Eleventh of September:
# A Call to Link Arms For
# All Young Americans_____ September 2001

American teenagers now share an experience with my Mother. It's one I have spent a lifetime trying to understand, and never could. But in one horrific moment last week, every young American grasped it.

Just as my Mom heard it when she was eighteen, word that our nation was under attack reached today's young as they sat in a high school classroom. As with her generation, the ambivalence of youth suddenly and violently collided with life's seriousness of purpose. And like her, while they may consign their pain to a secret part of their being, today's teens shall forever view life's mysteries through a prism of tears shed too early.

If my Mother's generation lost its innocence at Pearl Harbor, then terrorism's ugly black bolt out of a clear blue sky took this generation's adolescence. Before last week, we were content watching "Survivor" on television. Now we pray for real ones to emerge. "Who Wants To Be A Millionaire" has given way to who among us wouldn't relinquish every penny if it would restore just one life.

Vanished along with the World Trade Center was a self-absorbed nation. And its wake has bestowed on every young American an obligation and an opportunity. Their task is to hold fast to those institutions and practices that render America unique. And their chance is to expand the idea of public service, and thus breathe new life into what it means to be an American.

In the process, which may take until that time when today's teens comb gray hair, this generation of young Americans will define us, our nation, and our sense of community for perhaps centuries to come.

In the short term, America's youth can meet their obligation by insisting that our nation's coming actions do not diminish our standing as a democracy governed by the rule of law. Retaliation creates endless retribution. Justice produces peace.

Then they must aggressively engage in public matters and commit to public service. And they can begin by knowing our own community and all of its diverse citizens. Western New York includes members of over two dozen faiths, including several of mid-eastern origin. So a good first step in understanding different cultures and religions around the world is to reach out and understand ourselves.

In coming years, young people must as well re-invent the notion of heroic service. And in the bravery of those who stopped one hijacked jet from reaching its target, they have a high standard to which they can aspire.

As with all life transforming events, these attacks produced new heroes and affirmed old ones. Fire fighters plunging headlong up the steps of exploding towers, as if ascending their own stairway to heaven, evokes both untold admiration and the realization that public service is not restricted to government work.

And husbands calling wives from doomed planes reflects the bonds and rewards of the most noble human service, that to family. Through the miracle of technology, the last people they spoke with were those they loved. Through the miracle of faith, the next person they spoke with was God.

In the time of Pearl Harbor, one of my Mother's heroes, Franklin Roosevelt, proclaimed four freedoms essential to the American experience: freedom of expression, to worship, from want, and from fear. By helping restore our freedom from fear, young Americans will insure that new life emerges from unspeakable loss, and that our brothers and sisters did not die in vain. ❖

# PERSONAL

## *Personal*

The home, having a domestic spirit of grace dwelling in it, should become the church of childhood. ❖

HORACE  BUSHNELL

Your children are not your children.   They are but arrows drawn from your bow.  And they live in the house of tomorrow, in which you can never dwell. ❖

KAHIIL  GIBRAN

## EDITOR'S NOTE ❖

The author has been blessed with remarkable family life and warm friendships. Some of his personal memories are related here by a master storyteller.

# FATHERS, FAMILY, AND
# ROBERT KENNEDY_____ June 1993

Robert Kennedy's youngest child, Rory, was born after he died. On evenings when her mother was unable to take her, we would ride together on my bicycle up Hyannisport's Sunset Hill to watch the magic of day dissolve into night.

At age five, blonde and beautiful, Rory possessed an independence and bravery that struck even her mother, Ethel, as remarkable. On family sailing picnics (usually made up of 10 or 15 children, Ethel, me, and enough peanut butter and jelly to coat the entire hull), Rory did virtually everything the older children did except permit anyone to assist her over the transom when climbing on board after a swim. When sudden storms overtook us and banished everyone below, Rory remained on deck with her mother and me, her face visible through damp towels that wrapped and separated her from piercing breeze. She was at once a fiercely willed and utterly serene child. And she was my favorite.

On the steep hills of Arlington Cemetery last Sunday evening, a human sea of moist eyes and reconciled hearts stood in tribute to Rory's father, their own fathers, and, somehow, the loss inherent in human plight. Looking upon their faces, I thought of children whose father had gone, those who shall lose theirs, and those who never even get to see their father, and wept.

As President Clinton rose to speak, my mind's eye saw mothers and children gathered at another burial site just up the river but almost 150 years removed in Gettysburg. Their fallen sons and fathers had also given what Abraham Lincoln called that day "the last full measure of devotion." Borrowing from and improving upon the thoughts of the Greek statesman Pericles (one of Robert Kennedy's heroes), Lincoln spoke of the living that would spring from the dead. He contrasted the inadequacy of words to consecrate a ground that men of valor had already rendered sacred, with his obligation to carry on their unfinished work. And he spoke of the fitting and proper nature of their pausing to dedicate in Pennsylvania, just as Pericles had in Peloponnesia over a thousand years ago.

As has been discussed in works of considerable scholarship, Robert Kennedy left much unfinished work. Arthur Schlesinger, Jr.'s seminal biography, informed by his theory of alternating ages of reform and conservatism in American political life, most accurately places Kennedy in that narrative.

But beyond Robert Kennedy's public achievements, it always seemed to me that examination of his political career misses the essential element of his being: as with all heroic Americans, he considered devotion to family to be the highest form of public service. And during my brief time with them, I came to see his devotion reflected in the adoration and esteem in which his wife and children held him. Indeed, if other fallen heroes belong to the ages, perhaps Robert Kennedy belongs to those of fierce independence and passion, like that of his daughter, Rory.

From the time that Ethel Kennedy first drove to the Hyannis Airport to pick me up, through her once bailing me out of jail for riding a motor scooter a bit too swiftly past a town policeman, and even after her well intentioned parental approval of me forever doomed whatever small chance I had of impressing her daughters of datable age, I have never known a woman of more kindness and joy. It was easy to see how her beauty, humor, and vibrancy caught her husband's eye.

Based on chats with his brother, sisters, and Ethel, during which my curiosity may have exceeded my tact, I suspect that Robert Kennedy possessed many of the attributes ascribed to him by admirers and detractors alike. And over the years, through a proud friendship with some of the children he cherished, I came to a visceral sense of his essence, perhaps best illustrated in a videotape commonly shown in television documentaries of the Kennedy era.

A presidential helicopter lands on a Cape Cod lawn, and from its enormous side emerges President John Kennedy. As a rush of children races to greet the arriving group, your eye can't help but follow the quiet grace of the distinguished president. But if your view remains on the helicopter steps,

Robert Kennedy appears. Reacting to the energy and glee of the children at just the sight of him, he falls to his knees to embrace them, and disappears inside a swirl of joy and love.

And as I stood on Arlington's hill, among the statesmen and soldiers who lie in silent tribute to the resiliency of the human spirit that endures their loss, I lamented that I had no children of my own to whom I might pass on such sentiment.

But as dusk turned to twilight, I realized that if we grasp the imperative of humanity to which Robert Kennedy devoted his life, we recognize our bond with and obligation to all who follow us. ❖

# World War and Baby Boomers: Promise Kept and Miles To Go

August 1995

Day after day, one by one, they leave us.

Their promises to us kept, our parents' generation is slipping away. With them they take first hand knowledge of a world at war. And they leave us behind, the demographic bulge still called the "post war baby boomers" as the bridge generation to a younger era for which World War II will never be anything but faraway history.

A couple of weeks ago, it was a retired Trico executive from Cheektowaga, who had occupied Japan with the Army's 1st Cavalry; a few days later, a retired North Buffalo heating executive who had received the Purple Heart for valor under fire in New Guinea. According to the notices, their wives of 44 and 48 years survive them — just as women their age endured when they were teenagers and high school sweethearts were taken forever.

Few generations get to symbolize, let alone create, an age. Our parents did both. And they are our last link to a certain kind of past where our real roots lie, an American Century now receding.

As 20-somethings, all they had left of some of their friends were names on an Honor Roll in front of the Kenmore Municipal Building or the Clarence Town Park. But they seemed less concerned with memorials and more with getting on. Perhaps they made promises, in the Bastogne snow or on Iwo Jima sand, that we, the children to come, would be living memorials to the sacrifice of those who died.

And more than we realize — from the ground we walk, the homes we loved, and the parenting we received — their war would shape us.

When we arrived, with a healthy economy permitting Mom to stay home while Dad changed the world, we were privileged from the first. We would have a childhood. We would go to high school.

Our Promethean fathers and angelic mothers erected for us shining castles under bright skies. From our hospital births, we were brought home to Levitt-inspired structures designed for young families. Under intense pressure to meet exploding post-war demands, developer Bill Levitt skipped the slow and complex step of building a basement, thereby denying many of us even the ancient right to a scary underground room until our parents traded up in the suburbs.

My father served as an Army courier in the war, flying air missions between the states and Europe. Like most veterans turned dads, he rarely discussed his overseas experiences. But despite his stoic reluctance to talk about war, as we grew older we could discern their deep effect through his determination to create a peaceful environment for us.

Huddled together in our playroom by the lake, which my father called the S.S. Happiness, the seven children in my family sailed with Puff the Magic Dragon without a trace of care. There'd be enough of that to come, he quietly explained. My parents even had a rule that no child could attend a funeral until the age of 18.

Yet "the war" was still an event that we understood as real and monumental. Our language and culture reflected it. Before "dugouts" housed heroic baseball players, they hid Japanese snipers. Before a ship called the "Enterprise" carried Kirk and Spock where no man had gone before, it carried Admiral Halsey and his boys to liberate American pilots held in Tokyo zoos.

When Mick Jagger described Satanic behavior, he "rode a tank in the General's rank, when the Blitzkrieg came and the bodies stank."

From the perspective of a new century, our own war, Vietnam, will be seen as an inevitable outgrowth of our parents'. As Robert McNamara now discloses, mental newsreels of Chamberlain capitulating to Hitler at Munich played over and over in the minds of the 1960's wise men. The trillions of dollars and thousands of lives they invested in elusive dominoes forever changed us.

And World War left us, of course, one legacy which no one could shield us from — the flash of atomic destruction that reflected for decades in our parents' anxious eyes and, often, our own.

❖

A playmate with whom I learned to walk later sat his 20's away in a Baltic Sea submarine monitoring Russian movements. I often think of him as the loneliest if not the coldest of warriors.

Yet, overall, our parents succeeded in giving us a life better than their own had been. We were spared depression and war.

If, as Yeats believed, we spend our adult lives searching for the same sense of security with which our parents provided us, my generation surely faces an impossible task. Our parents set out to prolong our innocence to offset the early loss of their own. And they succeeded.

It was our parents who lived the century's defining time. Through those who remain, we can still touch it. Our task, when they are gone, is to ensure that our own children comprehend it. ❖

# A Merry, Buffalo Christmas

December 2001

During the holidays, my parents filled our family home with music. Their collection of LP's for Easter, the Fourth of July, and Saint Patrick's Day would emerge in season and supplant the daily dose of Broadway musicals with which we seemed to end each evening.

None of us seven children possessed anything approaching musical talent or understanding. But by tying our daily life to its uplifting presence, my parents gave us the gift of being moved by music.

And no musical canon meant more to us then, or evokes more today, than Christmas carols. We all have our favorite, mine being "Have Yourself a Merry Little Christmas." And in this year's most joyous season, ending a most sorrowful year, for perhaps the first time I understand why.

Composer Hugh Martin and lyricist Ralph Blane wrote "Have Yourself a Merry Little Christmas" in late 1943, in the midst of World War II. To my teenage ears in the 1960's, its understated tone set it apart from its more brassy brethren, and provided an intimate expression of an already over-commercialized holiday.

And its somber references to troubled times reflect the era in which it was written. But like Frank Capra's classic cinematic equivalent, "It's a Wonderful Life," the song's dark approach to the season of light ultimately gives rise to a powerful assertion of hope.

"Have Yourself a Merry Little Christmas" reached its popular height during Christmas, 1944. As war's end finally seemed within reach, that December brought awful news of Adolph Hitler's final, desperate offensive. In what would be called the Battle of the Bulge, thousands of American boys were trapped in Bastogne, Belgium, freezing to death in the snow or being slaughtered by enemy forces. To ease their suffering, some American soldiers used their helmets to render wounded friends unconscious.

❖

At home, it was a particularly grim and frigid December. While impoverished Buffalo residents searched city streets for firewood, a milk shortage compelled Mayor Joseph E. Kelly to ban its consumption by anyone but infants. And when news of our boys' plight in Bastogne reached stateside, the thought of holiday joy became all but unbearable.

On the radio, Blane's muted lyrics implored citizens to "let your heart be light," and promised that "from now on, our troubles will be far away." And war weary Americans felt they'd somehow been given permission to feel optimism and warmth.

Hearing the song some twenty years later and surrounded by their children, my parents pensive quiet would unwittingly interpret the work for us, as the melody took them back to their own youth in that dark December. My mother noticed that by the time we heard it, the song's prayerful lament that "we'll have to muddle through somehow" had been replaced by cheerier sentiment. And she told us how lucky we were not to know a holiday season like that of 1944.

But now we know. For thousands of Americans with an empty chair at the holiday meal this year, and thousands others with loved ones overseas, the song again resonates as we yearn for days when our troubles will be gone.

We think of the seven Western New York families forever torn asunder by terrorism in this tragic American autumn, and we wonder if our hearts can ever again be light.

But inspired by those who went before us in even darker days, and lifted by the life affirming nature of music, we remember those taken from us, give thanks for the holiday we have, and hope for better ones to come. ❖

# AUSTIN MCCRACKEN FOX
# MEMORIAL SERVICE
*Westminster Episcopal Church* ❖ *Buffalo, New York*
_____ December 30, 1996

In ancient Greece, when men of wisdom and high achievement passed on, citizens believed that the gods were jealous.

Through intellect and insight, the deceased had revealed too much of the mystery of life, thereby treading in god-like achievement. And in a fit of envy, the Greeks consoled themselves, Olympus took their hero before he spread even more joy and comfort.

As we approach the dawn of mankind's twenty-first enlightened century, that by our faith we know this is not true, does little to lessen our loss, or diminish our notion that today in the heavens, the council of learned men and women relish the prospect of experiencing that which we have: the privilege of learning at the side of Austin Fox.

In this season of Christmas lights and Hanukkah candles, affirming the birth of our Lord and marking renewed life at the temple of Jerusalem, we celebrate the imperfect human impulse to extend ourselves, to give to one another.

It is fitting and proper, then, that together we offer someone whose generosity of spirit and joy of living bestowed so much on so many.

And chief among his gifts was knowledge.

To several generations of Western New Yorkers, Mr. Fox revealed the pursuit of knowledge as noble; its possession, enriching; and its sharing, an essential component of love.

He accomplished this task through mythic presence and stunning intellect. But as his great friends and cherished family know, his dashing features and elegant bearing belied an enchanting, ironic humor that transcended the years separating student and teacher.

Along with his colleagues, Mr. Fox looked upon the duties of educator as a sacred trust — a temporary, careful holding of young minds in trust for the benefit of Buffalo parents and American future.

If at mid-century you thought Tinker to Evans to Chance was nifty work, you would have marveled at The Nichols School triple play of Sutter to Sessions to Fox.

And while those boys of summer merely flipped a baseball, these men of autumn — Millard Sessions, Albert Sutter, and Austin Fox — shaped minds and sculpted souls, in jaunty style, with quick wit, and a subtle tip of a cap to parents cheering their every move.

In our years of fragile intellect and temperament, they granted us safe passage to our adult selves, provided us safe harbor from adolescent storms, and crafted us into safe bets that someday, in some small way, we might help carry the burdens of tomorrow.

When Mr. Fox recited the passion of a romance poet, you yearned for a beloved to have and to hold. And when he exalted the words of a heroic poet, you were desperate to be gallant in her service.

And as with all great historians — Gibbon's musings on the Roman Empire, Tocqueville's evocation of infant America, and Shelby Foote's depiction of the horror of Civil War — when Austin Fox spoke of Ellicott's urban planning, Olmsted's vision, or McKinley's final hours, you'd swear that he was describing people he knew and events he experienced.

And through the miracle of human imagination, perhaps he was.

Mr. Fox applied his Jeffersonian breadth of learning far beyond education, participating as well in our civic religion of public affairs. And he did so blessed with what Emerson called the "anxiety of influence," engaging the same caliber of thought, critical analysis, and compassion that informed his academic life.

President John Kennedy once said that if more politicians understood poetry, and more poets understood politics, this world would be a better place in which to live.

❖

Austin Fox understood both, and struggled mightily to fuse the empathetic spirit of one into the activist nature of the other. And I like to think that in one rather insignificant public servant in the County of Erie, he succeeded.

At the center of the German literary tradition lies the Bildungsroman, the story of early development or spiritual education of a main character.

And as we look back on this, the American century, and the exceptional life of Austin Fox that both spanned and defined it, we realize that both man and nation came of age together.

As both an American baby boomer and a student of Mr. Fox, then, countless others and I were twice blessed. Reared in a peace and prosperity born of the despair of depression and the horror of war — that he and his generation endured — we experienced the thrill of safe travel and adventure around the world.

And under his guidance, we learned that no journey is as enriching or enlightening as one on which a good book takes us.

But it was for his children that he reserved his most precious gifts.

To Stephen, he gave a passion for their heritage, and the special joy derived from music and the performing arts.

With Susan, he shared devotion to both the treasure of books and the magic spell that children cast over us all.

In Sally, he instilled the sacred nature of human labor, and the knowledge that it both precedes and produces capital.

On Cindy, he conferred appreciation of language from every culture, and the joy of instructing others in all its nuance.

And to his beloved wife, Jean, he gave everything.

To be in his presence, then, was to at once touch Western New York's past and its future. With care and affection, he taught us from whence we came, secure in the conviction that it would help us in reaching where we want to go.

In several generations, Austin Fox ignited the flame of knowledge.

Guided by that light, his students ventured forth to distinguish themselves in education, medicine, law, commerce, the written word, and the performing arts.

Here at home, throughout our nation, and, indeed, around the world, these men and women have not only made a difference, they have made it better.

In their souls, the flame of learning burns brightly, never to be extinguished, as they spread more knowledge and wisdom with the dawn of each new day.

And no mere endeavor of ours, be it urban planning, waterfront development, or growing commerce, shall bring more honor to our region, than the warmth of those eternal flames, ignited by Austin Fox so long ago, that now light the world. ❖

# Vincent M. Gaughan, Sr.
# Mass of Christian Burial

*Our Lady of Victory Basilica* ❖ *Lackawanna, New York*

January 8, 1993

As Homer, the poet of heroes, tells us, there exists in the evening sky two types of stars: those that swiftly shoot across the horizon, blinding us with their brief but stunning light. And those that through their long and dependable presence, and seemingly endless energy, transfix us, and create in their space a light that remains long after the star has gone out.

My Father was of this second type of star. And when he directed the force of his warmth and light on you, he somehow lifted you beyond yourself as you basked in and surrendered to the energy and enthusiasm of his light source.

In his lyrical, Celtic grace, he thought he would live forever. And as it turns out, he shall.

Lawyers, once, were children, wrote Charles Lamb. And if you require proof of that assertion, you need look no further than my father. In language, thought, vision, and laughter, he was the essence of youth. And children, his kindred spirit, danced under his magic spell.

And his was a uniquely American life. More than any other that we might summon to mind, my Father's journey from 28 Downing Street to advisor in our land's highest office, defined the America that each of us has come to know.

He loved this nation, and in particular, its single defining idea of eternal experiment. He rejoiced in its success, pondered its ills, and wept at its shame.

But to fully comprehend my Father's dedication to forming a more perfect union, you must see its connection to his love of family. As with so many of you of his generation here this morning, my Father saw his family and his country as directly related. To him, each of our families serve as parent of our nation, responsible for its fate, able to shape its destiny, and therefore compelled to assist it in the name of love.

Returning home from Europe after a long separation from his family, the composer, John Phillip Sousa, whose work my father loved, wrote "The Stars and Stripes Forever" on the deck of his ship, in celebration of reuniting with wife and children. As my Father was so fond of reminding us, it was not flag, but family, that inspired such an intimate burst of joy.

My Father took great pride in the fact that he was born on June 14, Flag Day. And as another of his favorite songs exclaims, "My county 'tis of thee, sweet land of liberty," I hear my Father's refrain: "Let family ring."

Let family ring, and compassion is sustained. Let family ring, and love will endure. Let family ring, and freedom shall follow.

As my Mother and he raised us, the centerpiece of their life was the children's playroom by the lake. Replete with nautical flags, porthole windows, captain's quarters, and ship's tiller, my Father called it the "S.S. Happiness."

And as those of us who loved him take him to his final resting place today, I must assure you that because of him, together or apart, in our own homes or on different continents, we are still sailing on that ship. And all her flags are flying. And family is her name. ❖

# SPEECHES

*Speeches*

## EDITOR'S NOTE ❖

In advancing his civic work, the author has addressed numerous groups in Buffalo Niagara and throughout America. The speeches selected here set forth his vision for Western New York in the new century.

# Chautauqua Conference on Regionalism
# Opening Address————————— June 1, 1997

When this century was three years old — that time in which everything in American life was new, and anything was possible — President Theodore Roosevelt invited Booker T. Washington to the White House.

This gesture of humanity, the first African American to dine in "The Peoples' House," exalted the nation, and inspired legendary Rag composer Scott Joplin to create a song honoring Roosevelt's kindred spirit. Joplin called it, "The Strenuous Life."

Today, with but three years remaining in this, the American Century, if these giants of government, education, and culture could be with us this morning, it seems to me that they'd be pleased and proud of the steps we've taken to make our nation a more civilized and less hazardous place in which to live.

But I suspect that they would as well be perplexed and disappointed with the injustice, inhumanity, and disparity of opportunity that continue to haunt the American experience.

For too many Americans, in my city of Buffalo, in Chautauqua, and in regions throughout our nation, it has indeed been a strenuous life. And the degree to which our manner of self-government impedes efforts to reduce suffering and create equality of opportunity is the degree to which we have failed.

It is these challenges that beckon us, and for these reasons that we convene here at Chautuaqua, informed by that singular American virtue of eternal experiment, to re-examine, re-think, and perhaps re-imagine the type of community we wish to live in and leave behind.

Eloquent women and men are about to speak the language of their craft: economies of scale; civic infrastructure; linked futures; and efficiencies of government. They all share the artist's gift of being able to speak that which we can only feel. And if you listen with care, you will discover that theirs is in truth the language of healing, of restoration of the larger self and higher purpose to which we aspired when, as individuals and as regions, we came of age so many years ago.

Each of us is here, then, in support of our community, in pursuit of better futures, and, somehow, in search of ourselves.

A hundred years ago, my region and its Buffalo centerpiece were ahead by a century. In intervening years, perhaps not unlike your hometown, we have endured difficult and painful changes, and today seem unable to regain proper course.

And yet, we continue firm in our conviction that there are stars in our path, knowing that which recommends us — to each other, our nation, and the world — remains vivid and strong.

As it turns out, then, our generation has an obligation and an opportunity. An obligation to acknowledge social, economic, and spiritual barriers that mid-century suburban growth inadvertently erected at century's end; and an opportunity to reinvent American life through enlightened policies to dismantle them.

From Homer's Odysseus, through Mark Twain's Huck Finn, to Steven Spielberg's E.T., the journey of life is, in the final analysis, the story of our efforts to reach shore, to rest assured, to return home.

And with your presence here this week, you bear witness to both your community's and Western New York's re-dedication to this essential task: To find our way back, as individuals and communities, to a more inclusive, sustainable, and prosperous society.

Together, we invest social capital and individual spirit, to re-establish alliances and prepare for unknown challenges that await us as the world's first truly multi-cultural society. And I submit to you that our cause is noble, our abilities great, and our interests common and united.

In the course of crafting this conference, I have in recent months thought a great deal about the American Dream. And it seems to me that it has always depended on who was doing the dreaming.

Our forefathers dreamt of freedom from tyranny, and they gained it. Our grandparents dreamt of freedom from the horror of world war, and they ended it. And today our new urban minorities — those of African, Asian, Hispanic, Latino, and Vietnamese origin — dream of the same beneficence that was bestowed on us of Polish and German and Italian and Irish descent when we first arrived.

And the true measure of our age will be whether we give it.

As we approach a new century, we encounter an age in which we must now dream with our eyes open. The ideas that we are about to hear, discuss, and test will inform those aspirations with firm basis and sound beginnings, so that our dreams might someday come to pass. ❖

# Chautauqua Conference on Regionalism in Education Opening Address_____October 27, 1999

Perhaps more than you shall ever know, I am pleased to be here, proud to be an American, and on this typically soft Chautauqua autumn evening, thrilled to be a Western New Yorker.

If, as the Greeks define it, happiness is expending all of your energy and intellect in a worthy cause, then I'm about the happiest guy in Buffalo Niagara. For the past fourteen months, I've had the privilege of traveling this nation, meeting with and learning from many of these uniquely American minds from whom you shall hear, and attempting to grasp the nature and practice of those of you engaged in humankind's most precious undertaking — bestowing the gift of knowledge on another.

As some of you may have heard, in an attempt to get us all in the proper spirit, I consolidated some of my internal organs last week. My doctor thought the gesture a bit over the top, but this particular organ wanted out, shall we say, quickly. So they gave me some whiskey and a bullet, and I closed my eyes and thought of my old school.

I was grateful for all the kind wishes and as well generous words about the rapidity with which I left the hospital. But I have to tell you: I talked my way into Harvard University some years ago, and talked myself into the Ford Foundation for these conferences two years ago. So believe me, talking my way out of Buffalo General Hospital was nothing.

My physician — a magnificent man and old pal — heard my case about the need to get on with these proceedings, and let me go. When I asked if he thought he had any chance of keeping me, he replied, "nary an illusion."

To this worthy undertaking, then, I've given fourteen months, 2900 frequent flyer miles, some newly gray hairs, and one appendix.

In return, I've worked with and been enriched by the likes of Dan Bratton, our co-chairs Carol Lorenc and Tom Frey, my hero, Stan Lundine, Len Faulk, the affable Don Ogilvie, several close pals and volunteers patient enough to put up with me, and most important, our Conference Scholars from high schools throughout Western New York, who've had to endure my cornball humor.

Can you even dream of a better bargain?

Now, with but hours left in this, the American Century, we accept that in many ways we were destined to be here for our rendezvous with tomorrow. For if children are our glimpse at immortality, then their education is the medium by which we touch the future.

As we commence these discussions, we do well to acknowledge that our voices shall carry to other times, and our obligations flow to specific yesterdays and countless tomorrows.

From the settlers at Plymouth, whose first act was to establish a public school.

Through Thomas Jefferson's assertion that "any nation that expects to be ignorant and free expects what never was and what never will be."

To the young Abraham Lincoln, son of a forest dweller, who by light of a candle introduced himself to Shakespeare, Socrates, and Locke.

On to Chautauqua's founders, whose paramount purpose in creating this national treasure was to educate tomorrow's citizens as a way of repaying yesterday's.

And finally, to your colleagues earlier in this century, who in response to a changing economic landscape realized that the American adolescent must no longer toil in a field, but rather in a classroom.

By each of their presence and being, we were bound to be here this evening, to address the one public policy that shall forever unite us: the imperfect, human impulse to reveal the pursuit of knowledge as noble; its possession, enriching; and its sharing an essential component of love.

To those who came before, and bestowed on us this education system that stands as an eloquent expression of mankind's highest aspirations, we owe our vigilance and care. As its temporary stewards, we eagerly accept the challenge to preserve its strengths and prepare it for new and difficult realities.

And to those young pupils who come after, we must explain how in our lifetime we permitted the harshness of inequity to touch any child, let alone an impoverished one, and imagine some way to craft new approaches worthy of them and posterity.

And as we speak to the ages, we must keep faith with the American tradition by which we define ourselves. That is, for those of us least able to achieve our dream and most vulnerable to unkind forces, there shall always be a door open to improve our mind, enrich our soul, and create more sustainable self. In our culture, that is education — easily accessible, safely administered, and joyously rendered.

With your presence here, you demonstrate your faith in youth and its energy as the ground-level condition of democracy. And you affirm that as we seek to shape their minds and sculpt their souls in this new age of collaboration, no man, no woman, no government, no institution, and now no school district can be an island.

And in honestly addressing those failings that afflict our system and thus beckon us here tonight, we say to ourselves and our nation: we think it need not be so, and we know that eventually it shall not be so.

So let history record that in the spirit of both the Chautuaqua and American experience, as the century turned, our minds were not on today's hardships, but tomorrow's promise; that we thought not of our own small challenges, but of our children's larger purpose; and that in the name of those who struggled mightily to grant this nation safe passage into its adult self, we began the awesome task of caring for a new American offspring.

Let this new age begin right here, right now, here in magnificent upstate New York; where east coast sophistication meets mid-western charm; where in man-made and God-given gifts we are without parallel; and in fiercely family-oriented ethos, without peer.

And where, to more effectively and equitably share the power of knowledge, we created the first American region without boundaries — not geographic ones to separate us, economic ones to divide us, or racial ones to diminish us.

Together now, as we light the flame of knowledge in ourselves and our children, we know that no other public endeavor shall bring us more honor than the warmth of this light, never to be extinguished, that can surely light the world. ❖

In this uplifting speech, the author proposes education reforms to increase equality of opportunity for urban and suburban school children.

# LEADERSHIP BUFFALO "LEADERSSPEAK.NOW" INAUGURAL SERIES; WNY PUBLIC BROADCASTING STUDIOS———November 30, 1999

Thank you very much, Mr. Conorozzo. That introduction was much too kind, far too generous, and filled with way too many lies. And while I didn't believe a word of it, I can tell by the look on my Mother's face, down here in the second row, that she believed every syllable.

Here we are in this most wondrous space of public television where, through the fusion of moving images and original ideas, the human condition is evoked and celebrated in all its pathos and glory.

And as well, where our own Mark Russell, with satire and song, reveals the central truths of public affairs and human folly. It's a privilege, and a bit of an adventure, to stand here with you tonight.

So to start right in: who here wants to make our magnificent City of Buffalo a brilliant, vibrant, American urban center, say aye.

Who wants our new century to begin with our public treasures restored and our city schools strengthened to be among our nation's best, say aye.

And who wants this unique region of Buffalo Niagara — which for centuries past has stood without peer — to be included in tomorrow's success stories, say aye.

Well, my work here is done.

Oh, just one more: who here tonight never wants to see that ad with my ugly mug on it that the Buffalo News has been endlessly running to promote this evening, say aye! I mean, come on, it's beginning to spook me and I can only image its effect on the innocent and unsuspecting.

You know the great story of Abraham Lincoln and how he described photographs of himself that revealed his rough edges as "painfully accurate." He

146
❖

loved to tell about the time he was approached by a stranger who claimed to have something that belonged to Lincoln. "But how can that be, " Lincoln asked, "we've never met before." And taking a pocketknife from his coat, the stranger explained that many years before he'd been given the knife with the instruction to hold onto it until he met someone uglier than he. "And I do believe, sir," the man told Lincoln, "that this knife belongs to you."

And that wonderful retort with which Lincoln replied when in their historic debates Stephen Douglas accused him of being "two-faced" on the matter of states rights. Turning to the audience, Lincoln asked, "I leave it to you: if I had another face do you really think I'd be walking around with this one?'

Leadership Buffalo Executive Director, Susan Russ; Mr. Conorozzo, Clare Root, who produced this evening, and my friend Pete Loehr of Buffalo State, who initiated this series; Honorable Jack Curtin; Catherine Schweitzer, and most important, Buffalo citizens, who've struggled mightily to advance and enrich the life of our community: as I am unsuited to stand on this beautiful performance stage, I'm as well unqualified to address the nature of leadership.

But I am grateful for the opportunity to discuss, and I hope in some small way, advance our cause of strengthening our city and preparing our region for the future we deserve.

And I'm grateful for the friendship and kindred spirit of Susie Russ. I may know little about the principles of leadership, but I do know that Susie has bestowed on our community, again in Lincoln's words, humankind's most precious gift, the gift of labor. So I can offer a three-word definition of leadership, Susan Warren Russ.

And while Susie's been misguided in her kind invitations to me to participate in Leadership Buffalo endeavors, it is fitting and proper that she asked me here this evening. For it is women public and community servants throughout America who are leading our age of regionalism. I've tried to learn everything I can about this new mode of inclusive and collaborative governance, and is some small way, promote its practice here.

As Joseph Campbell, the brilliant theologian and author of the "The Power of Myth," wrote, perhaps we cannot all be heroes, but in our lives, we can all have heroic passages. And each of the Western New Yorkers I just mentioned, in many instances echoing the lives of beloved parents who went before, have already established their heroic passages, and our task is but to follow them.

As for me and my knowledge of leadership, you should have no illusions. I know next to nothing about it. A bit, perhaps, about marshaling divergent views toward a common goal. And as a student of history, a little about the qualities found in those who led this American experiment ever upward.

Not all readers can be leaders, Harry Truman once wrote, but all leaders must be readers. As did my Father — who served three American presidents, including Mr. Truman — I've taken that sentiment to heart, and believe that found in our past are insights and inspirations with which to grasp our future.

If you got close enough to Thomas Jefferson, you could hear just under his breath a melody he constantly hummed to himself, which charmed his admirers and annoyed his critics. Read virtually any story of an encounter with Lincoln, and you'll discover the almost transcendent serenity he exuded that comforted all who came into his presence. And find a contemporary account of Theodore Roosevelt, who with a bang and a wallop opened this century we're about to close, and you inevitably come across the descriptive words "enormous" and "large" — quite something for a man who stood only five feet, seven inches tall.

These heroes shared, in endless quantity, an energy and passion for life, unyielding commitment to serve something other than themselves, a refusal to waste even a moment doing it, and irrepressible joy, arrived at, in many instances, only after enduring unspeakable sorrow.

Each fiercely loved their nation and their community. And I like to think that all of them would be interested in and proud of the large ideas of self-government we've created these past two centuries, and the rather small ideas we shall discuss this evening.

❖

It's been said that only six degrees of separation exists between every human being on God's earth. But for those of us fortunate enough to be Americans, and blessed enough to be Western New Yorkers, I believe there are perhaps two degrees, and in truth, only one. In essence, that's what this broad and exciting doctrine of regionalism asserts. That in interests and aspirations, we are as close as our compassion permits — distinguished only by those unique imperfections and frailties that render our souls joyously human.

And linking every public policy by which we govern ourselves to our common origin and shared future, is the challenge to which regionalism beckons us. There's an ancient English expression that we live in each other's shadow. To which we as Americans would add that, as well, we bask in each other's light. In these brief thoughts this evening, I hope to illustrate how regional thinking can assist us in achieving this, humanity's indispensable purpose. And one of the tools with which to accomplish this is a strong urban education system, about which I'd like to offer some ideas in a moment.

For some time now in our reform journey, we've been overwhelmed with complex ideas and simple truths. And the net effect is we're left wondering, what is regionalism, and why is it important to our community? To grasp its full meaning, and understand its essential importance to Western New York, we must go back to the 1960's, when regionalism first emerged only twenty short years into a post-war boom that gave rise to its origin.

As with so many other transforming events or ideas throughout our nation's history, the concept of regional thinking has been around for some time. Just as Thomas Jefferson first wrote the phrase, "preserving the union" — that's right, Mr. Lincoln borrowed it from him; and Franklin Roosevelt was the first president to devote a White House foreign policy meeting to a small country called Viet Nam, the first reference I could find to regionalism as we define it today was uttered by Lyndon Johnson in a 1965 address to the National Urban League.

The mid-sixties had seen the first fissures in the uniquely American version of successful city life. And urban policy planners were beginning to recognize the ill effects that the even more uniquely American idea of subur-

149
❖

ban freedom was imposing on our great urban centers.

Indeed, let's for a moment travel even further back to the inception of this, the American Century, that time celebrated these past months in a Toronto theater in the musical, "Ragtime." To that time when American cities were entire worlds, everything was new, and anything was possible. And that magic spirit — concentrated, as we all know, and as the writer Lauren Belfer has so elegantly reminded us in her recent book, "City of Light," right here at our Pan American Exposition — under which America's melting pot was entranced.

In that rag time, all that we desired, aspired to, or dreamt of, could be found in our still infant democracy's leveling impulse that cast greatly affluent, immigrant poor, and average worker all within a few city blocks of one another.

But by mid-century, shining cities had dulled, masonry darkened, and the melody of sad rags prevailed. And American middle class wealth and Henry Ford-given mobility began to evoke visions of ever-larger surroundings.

And then came war.

And with it, an assault on an entire race that placed humanity's existence at risk, and compelled giant heroes, disguised as young American boys, to climb out of small boats off Omaha Beach and embark on their journey into the ages. And those who left their teen-aged friends in Bastogne snow or on Iwo Jima sand, they made solemn promises to themselves, that their children would live long and joyous lives, sheltered by freedom's protection from fear, want, loneliness, and harm.

Some of these men and women — who saw high school friends become names on town park monuments or VFW photographs — they're still with us.

But as we learn in daily newspaper notices, they will not be here forever. So go to them now and ask, and they'll abandon their stoic nature and quietly explain the impetus that compelled them to wrap some of us in the cocoons we would come to know as suburbs. For upon their return, that's where they sought to fulfill those whispered promises made to fallen friends.

❖

Aided by GI Bills, Levitt houses, inadvertent or purposefully racist lending policies, and a booming economy that laid down more concrete, lit more darkness, and developed more rural land than mankind had ever witnessed, our parents sought comfort in the idea of working in one place, and living in quite another.

And they did it for us.

For a period it worked. But public resources began to disappear, urban populations dwindled, numbers of political sub-divisions grew, and suburban towns and villages and their governments became more independent and isolated. They began to compete aggressively with each other for less and less revenue, all the while crowding out those left behind in the city, whose older assets required more expensive upkeep, and whose lesser affluence reduced their political influence.

So it was, then, in the 1960's that leaders first recognized that overlapping and fragmented local governments were harming rather than helping one another. And pretty soon, across America, after a day's work downtown, we Baby Boomers — now mothers and fathers ourselves — began arriving home from our abandoned past.

We were coming home from nowhere.

And when the Cold War ended, and Germany and Japan won by recognizing that political boundaries were dead, and the globe had become one marketplace, a second and equally compelling reason emerged for regions like ours to resuscitate our inner city, and dismantle those social and cultural barriers that over the years increasingly separated us. That is, our own economic survival in a brutally competitive world economy.

And so with this story, born of these sacrifices, and tempered by these harsh realities, we find ourselves here, on this lovely autumn evening, in support of our community, in pursuit of better futures, and somehow, in search of ourselves.

At this moment, regional thinkers throughout our nation are working across social, geographical, and racial boundaries; creating the essential alliance in American local government today — that between city and suburbs;

folding overlapping functions; planning sustainable growth; and creating equity in education. As gifted leaders, they speak the language of their craft: collaboration; inclusion; civic infrastructure; land use planning; and linked futures. And they all share the artist's gift of speaking that which we can only feel.

But if you listen with care, you discover that in truth, theirs is the language of healing; of restoration of the standard of larger self and higher purpose set by those who granted us safe passage to our adult selves; and a reaffirmation of the type of communities and neighborhoods that we wish to live in and leave behind.

And I submit that achieving the social, economic, and indeed, spiritual ends of regionalism, is the task that this broad sweep of American history has placed on our generation. Because our parents and grandparents protected and sustained this experiment in democracy, they made a difference. And now we must make it better.

So how do we accomplish this? I say by making Buffalo Niagara a place of bold, persistent experimentation and ideas. And by making solemn vows ourselves: that in the shaft of the new century's first light that is about to shine on us, fragmented government will meet its match. And under your leadership, and that of countless other concerned public and private groups and citizens, it shall meet its master.

In this spirit, permit me to offer a reform idea relating to our city, its schools, and public education throughout our region. Along with the privilege of seeing next month's new dawn, we must accept as well the responsibilities that accompany our rendezvous with tomorrow. We must let history record that as the century prepared to turn, we decided that in our small corner of America, unequal opportunity for any child was no longer acceptable.

To accomplish this, I propose the establishment of a Buffalo Regional Education Center, to include city and suburban schools, and that would oversee the joining of our city school district with the Board of Cooperative Services that has served our suburban districts since 1948. As an already existing regional entity that crosses all boundaries but our city line, BOCES has enhanced that quality of education in our suburban districts. And now it should be permitted to serve Buffalo.

Second, to cast these new and intriguing charter schools as a collaborative rather than competitive reform, I ask our Buffalo School District to open its own charter school. This way, our public educators see for themselves what potential charters hold. And to address the financing challenge, I propose that private vouchers rather than public funds pay for any Buffalo student who leaves a public school to attend a charter. This might level the uneven playing field that has created rancor between school districts and the charter schools from which they are intended to learn.

Finally, I think it's time that as a community, we determine a more fair and effective way to finance public education that does not leave our city's children in poor facilities, with poor resources, which lead to poor performance. And until we do, propose a formal system of relationships between affluent suburban districts and their inner city counterparts. With BOCES' ability to provide the transportation, a wide range of exchange programs and classes are possible.

We live in an age of freedom triumphant over powerful walls around the world. And yet here we permit old and petty barriers to continue to divide and diminish us. The essence of these small ideas of mine is that in our approach to educating our children, that can no longer happen. It's time to embrace new practices, and move on.

For now, with but hours left in this, the American Century, this time of opportunity for regions like our's to distinguish themselves, never has there been more fertile ground or urgent need for all of us to offer our thoughts and ideas as to how Western New York should look, and for what it should stand, after we're gone. And to accomplish this, each of us must accept our unique obligations.

We citizens must remain discontented, but not discouraged. To those who say that they'll give Buffalo Niagara two or three more years to shape up or they're shipping out, we say that we're not gong anywhere until we restore our region, its magnificent city, and its people restored to their rightful place. I for one can tell you that I'm not going anywhere until we see this through. Why we're just warming up, and we're having a pretty good time doing it.

To local elected servants reluctant to consider reform, we understand that government and politics is the art of the possible. But they must understand that leadership is the art of creating new possibilities. And utilizing the new tools of cooperation — regardless of their effect on their standing or influence — we now insist that they create this new potential.

The philosopher, Isiahah Berlin, whose intellect and essays defined humane values throughout much of this century, once wrote that the world was divided into two type of minds: hedgehogs, as he called them, who have one big idea; and foxes, who create many smaller ones. Among his foxes, Berlin counted Aristotle, Shakespeare, and Jefferson.

And while we Western New Yorkers may never be include in such company, the life of our collective mind did produce one magnificent idea. And we called it Buffalo.

In it we asked Frederick Law Olmsted to take nature's canvas, and lift our spirits. Form it sprung unique American voices, including Mark Twain, Scott Fitzgerald, and Joyce Carol Oates. Through it passed history's most daring expression of human freedom — the underground railroad — as people like Frederick Douglas and Harriet Beecher Stowe journeyed right through our City on the way to achieving freedom.

In its heart — in our own Niagara Square — Millard Fillmore came home; Abraham Lincoln attended services; Grover Cleveland practiced law; William McKinley lay in state as Theodore Roosevelt sketched in his diary a vision for his new century; Franklin Roosevelt set cornerstones; Harry Truman performed music; and in a visit to out city thirty-seven years ago this autumn, as he first learned of nuclear arms in Cuba after addressing a Buffalo crowd, John Kennedy pondered humankind's extinction.

On it we constructed the world's envy of man-made space. From Louis Sullivan's elegance to H.H. Richardson's majesty through Frank Lloyd Wright's vision and E.B. Green's wisdom, we have, in songwriter Paul Simon's lovely and lyrical phrase, "angels in the architecture, spinning in infinity, singing alleluia."

And perhaps most important, we filled our idea of the American city with an ethos and ethic of a fiercely family-oriented people, who love their children and make life choices in support of their interests. So if you need ask what brings us here this evening, in our nation's proudest tradition of advancing the civic good, it seems to me that it's this one degree of separation, if you will that binds us to those who shaped our story and created this enormous post-war American wealth in which we have prospered.

To this magnificent God-given and man-made landscape that we call home, I ask each of you to create a landscape of ideas as to how we might strengthen community, preserve that which makes unique, and aspire to something larger than ourselves.

While our parents and grandparents waged world war and suffered economic depression to meet their obligations, our task, to create enduring community, is perhaps less dramatic. But I suspect that if any one of them could be here with us this evening, they'd be the first to accept the job, and insist that we too embrace the challenge.

One hundred years ago, our region and its Buffalo centerpiece were ahead by a century. In intervening years, we've endured difficult and painful changes, and yet we continue firm in our conviction that there are stars in our path, knowing that which recommends us remains vivid and strong.

And in all of our voices extolling the virtues of leadership, perhaps we hear echoes of those Western New Yorkers who went before, imploring us to bear in mind this essential truth. Imploring this "me generation," as Tom Wolfe called us, to think through our legacy with care; and challenging we baby boomers, now in life's late afternoon and beginning to ponder the twilight, to ask: by what do we want to be remembered.

The 1960's failed promises? 1970's immersion in self? 1980's unspeakable greed? An end to both century and city for which the ages would surely condemn us? Or whether each of us will summon the spirit of this one, small degree of separation that in truth unites more than divides us; and in the name of humanity, sacrifice a bit of individual interest in order to advance a collective good. This journey shall be long and not without difficulty. But if it were easy I for one would not be so enthusiastic about embarking on it.

From Homer's Odysseus through Mark Twain's Huck Finn to Steven Spielberg's E.T., the journey of life is, in the final analysis, the story of our efforts to reach shore, to rest assured, to return home. And with your presence here this evening, you bear witness to Western New York's rededication to this essential task: to find our way back, as individuals and communities, to a more inclusive, sustainable, and prosperous society.

As for me, I once saw my modest work described in a magazine article as that of a good government advocate, or a "goo-goo" for short. And driving downtown tonight, I heard an old George Gershwin song — the one about the fellow whose frustration and utter madness of his latest love has ended, and his life was once again tranquil and normal. But, oh, he sings, "how I wish I was ga-ga again." We may not all be leaders, and we may not all be movers of humankind, but I promise you that I will always be a "goo-goo" who's forever "ga-ga" over Buffalo and Western New York.

As for us together, I believe that as Americans, when our time comes to give an accounting of our life's work, in addition to the other questions posed, we shall be asked, "What did you do with you freedom? Did you use it to help others become free?" And our true measure will be our answer.

Leadership is, for me, an invitation to be kind. It's the imperative to serve others, waste not a moment in so doing, be ever mindful of what Emerson called "the anxiety of influence," and embrace joy. It's not interested in tomorrow, but in countless tomorrows. It asks not, "who's got game," but rather "who's got next." And leadership compels us to leap from what we know to what we believe.

We know that old practices die hard, and we believe that they too shall pass. We know that boundaries are comfortable, but we believe that they will end. And we know our community is at risk, yet we believe it will endure.

To love athletics is to lift the spirit through motion.

To love the arts is to enrich the soul.

To love nature is to feel God's presence.

To love another is to see His face.

156
❖

But to love community, that's to be American.

And so tonight we have much to celebrate, and much work to do. I've been giving some thought lately to the heightened opportunities that the new century presents to everyone in this room. On December 31$^{st}$, at that stroke of midnight, all of us shall instantly become old, be from "the old century," be from yesterday. And that's why our standard and our bar and our responsibility is set so high, and our responsibility is to be as creative, innovative, and forward thinking as we can. Our times demand it. And I think that's exciting.

For perhaps the most remarkable news tonight is that we made it. Of all American cities, perhaps no other was treated more unkind by the 20$^{th}$ century than our own. As Langston Hughes' character, Simple, once exclaimed, "I have been shot, stabbed, wounded, held down, shut in, locked out, underfed, underpaid, under-loved, and everything but undertaken. But I and still here."

Well, we're all still here, and we say let's start this new century right here, right now. In this nation or world, there is no place like us, no sense of place to match us. Here in our region, where eastern sophistication meets mid-western charm, we have a thrilling story to tell.

It's a humane story. It's a heroic story. It's a fragile, tragic, resilient, redemptive, and ultimately triumphant story.

It's the Buffalo story. And together now, with pride, prayer, soul and spirit, let's tell and re-tell it to ourselves, our children, our nation, and the world.

Thanks very much. ❖

## EDITOR'S NOTE ❖

Two months after the destruction of the World Trade Center, Buffalo State College convened a conference on its future, and asked the author to address it. Sketching the imperative of sacrifice in public service, he connected the work of reviving Buffalo with his ideas of leadership, and that which is owed to those who were lost in the terrorists' attacks.

# BUFFALO STATE COLLEGE
# STRATEGIC PLANNING CONFERENCE
# KEYNOTE ADDRESS_____November 30, 2001

Thanks very much Dr. Howard, and good morning.

It's a privilege to be among such distinguished company this morning, and with such cherished friends. Muriel Howard is a warm and long-time friend of the Gaughan family, and I add my congratulations to her for convening this important discussion at this, our urban jewel of Buffalo State College, and thank her for extending me the privilege of participating.

My own academic career has been much on my mind this year as my college class celebrated our 25th reunion this past June. I considered attending the festivities — I'd never been to a reunion before — until I received the invitation, which read: "come join your Harvard pals as we celebrate the fact that your class of 1976 includes 3 Nobel prize winners, 4 Pulitzer Prize winners, 9 Academy Award recipients, 6 Tony Award winners, 14 Emmy Award winners, 6 members of the United States Congress, and the world's most gifted cellist."

The invitation went on to say, "and kindly fill in the blank below and tell us what you do."

After jotting down "regionalism expert," I somehow lost my enthusiasm for traveling to Cambridge.

But I can tell you that I wouldn't trade my work for all those accolades combined. And I can tell you as well that being a modestly known regional thinker does have its moments.

Why just a few weeks ago, I was in Wilson Farms on the corner of Elmwood and Auburn, standing in line and minding my own business when a typically kind and soft spoken elderly Western New York man came up to me and said, "you know, you look a lot like Kevin Gaughan." And I said, "yes, sir."

And he continued, "do a lot of people say that to you?"

And I said, "yes, sir."

And he said, "must make you mad."

The poet Kahiil Gibran once wrote, "Your children are not you children / they are but arrows sprung from your bows / and they dwell in the house of tomorrow / in which you can never live." So this morning, as we consider our city's and region's house of tomorrow, it is fitting and proper that we hold this discussion in your student union, as each of the questions before us relate to the Buffalo State of tomorrow, when today's students comb gray hair, another cycle of Americans follow, and my generation is no longer here.

What a joyous undertaking in which to participate — working not for ourselves, but rather for posterity. And this core spirit of the education profession — attempting to touch a tomorrow that we shall never see — is deeply embedded in regional thinking.

And it's a particular honor to be in this place of learning from which my Mother graduated, and where she first came to recognize the pursuit of knowledge as noble; its possession, enriching; and its sharing, an essential component of love. And I can tell you that she passed that belief onto each of her seven children, sixteen grandchildren, and four great-grandchildren.

When my Mother heard that I was to have the privilege of being with you this morning, she didn't ask what topic I was to discuss, or what ideas I'd offer. She only said, "for heaven's sake, Kevin, just be sure your hair is combed."

Those who went before us no doubt gathered to examine what changes and reforms would affect the future of our city and the region in which it rests. But never in such an important moment in our nation's narrative, and never toward such large purpose.

This tragic American autumn, with an assault on humanity we could never foresee, and a fiscal crisis we should have, informs the context in which we meet. "The unmentionable odor of death that offends the September night," as W.H. Auden wrote in his poem, "September 1939," shall linger for some time and permeate every public and private choice we make.

❖

In times like these, we do well to think of the Roman orator, Marcus Aurelius, who said that in any choice with which we are presented, prefer the hard. That holds good not only in great matters but in small ones as well — in "fighting by the frozen Danube, and in starting the day early."

I believe that just by choosing to make Buffalo Niagara our home, we've all passed the Aurelius test. Because enduring our local difficulties, and Lord knows there are many, sure as heck can be hard here.

But we welcome the challenge. And in the early light of this new century, with harsh sacrifices in front of us all, I hope to convey why we embrace this hard but wondrous choice.

If, as the ancient Greeks defined it, happiness is expending all of your energy and intellect in a worthy cause, then I'm the happiest guy in town. Because what could be a more worthy cause than our magnificent city and region, and preparing it for the future to which we all aspire, and we all deserve.

I trade in the currency of ideas, and my modest work seeks to reduce fragmented governance and restore a sense of shared community across those social, economic, racial, and geographic boundaries that purport to divide and diminish us. By the Aurelius standard is this work hard? A little. But I can tell you that it's the difficulty that makes it an adventure. And the adventure is what makes it fun.

My small work has brought me into contact with large minds throughout America, from whom I've learned much. And I've concluded that there exists two large and historic forces that, if we summon the courage to harness, can help us save our city and thus strengthen this institution.

And the first is regional reform and cooperation. When I began educating myself about regional thinking now about eight years ago, I did something my Father taught me. He always said that if you wanted to fully understand something, you had to see it for yourself.

So I got on a plane. I went over to Cleveland; I went down to Chattanooga; I went out to Portland, Oregon; and I went to Mecklenberg County and Charlotte, North Carolina — the place that's attracting so many of our children. All great places, with kind people. But they couldn't hold a candle to what we have here in Buffalo in man-made and God-given gifts. And yet, they're surging ahead, creating vibrant economies, and keeping their young people home with solid promises of bright futures.

Why? Because they shedding old practices and embracing new doctrines of collaborative leadership and inclusive governance.

Which leads to the question: what is regionalism? Why is it important? And how is it potentially helpful to us here in Western New York?

Here's my short-hand definition: Regionalism is the belief that by increasing cooperation among our county, city, towns, and villages, we can produce more effective and less costly government. And perhaps more important, we can produce a more sustainable, inclusive, and prosperous community. It's also, regionalism, a belief, that no body, no living thing can exist without a vibrant, beating heart. And in our instance, that's this magnificent City of Buffalo — which we all this morning know is in peril.

And finally, regionalism is a conviction that the passkey to success in this new century is all of ourselves working together across those social, economic, racial, and geographic boundaries that for too long have divided and diminished us.

And you should know that the regionalism movement sweeping the nation today is in response to two concurrent dynamics: one, post war suburban growth and its attendant explosion of local government layers and bureaucracies. In my research, the first reference to regionalism that I found was uttered by President Lyndon Johnson in a speech before the National Urban League in 1964. It was in the 1960's that urban policy planners first recognized that suburban governments were harming, not helping one another, competing for dwindling public funds and leaving behind city governments with their older assets and lesser influence.

Dynamic number two: the emergence of a brutally competitive global economy that demanded an end to local economic competition — Hamburg versus Clarence, Buffalo versus Amherst — and began the era of the region as the most effective economic operating unit.

❖

And there's a second force we must harness. As regionalism has grown, and as societies across America became truly multi-cultural — even in hinterland areas like our own — a second reform movement began tracking alongside regionalism. And that's the age of inclusive governance in which we've entered, the changing nature of local government and changing roles of its participants.

Think of the several large public policy challenges with which we've been confronted here in Buffalo Niagara in the last five years: whether to build a new Peace Bridge; a new convention center; if we should move the Buffalo Zoo; whether we would permit Albany bureaucrats to bury the one national treasure to which Buffalo lays sole claim, our Commercial Slip; or whether Children's Hospital should be moved.

Take any one of those issues, and you'd be hard pressed to name what position any politician took on it. Why? Because public officials don't take public positions anymore, they don't consider it part of their jobs. And they've created a leadership vacuum which foundations, academics, businessmen, and yes, average citizens, must now fill. That's an exciting and far-reaching opportunity.

In this new encounter of interests, there's a rapidly changing standard of inclusion. The public policy decision-making table is being transformed into one that's larger, more round, less white male, and more reflective or our diverse community.

And perhaps most important, the imperative of crafting a transparent decision-making process. "Transparency," meaning visible, touchable, and able to be affected by all, is the buzzword with the most sizzle in local reform efforts. It's essential to creating consensus, leading to decision, and producing action. Think about it, if any of the policy decisions over which we've recently struggled came before Western New York a decade ago, the decision would have been made by about eight white guys behind a closed door at a private club. But today we're all involved. We're exhaustively contributing. And it turns out it's a pain in the neck. It's challenging, difficult, and time-consuming. We've given re-birth to a basic democratic tenet: only from open clashes of special interests can the public interest emerge.

❖

We're in the early stages of this movement in Buffalo Niagara. We've experienced small triumphs. But like an awkward teen who, after years of little growth, feels sprouting limbs and raging hormones that are driving us nuts, and making us question whether becoming a mature community is worthwhile. Well it is. We must hold firm to this inclusive process. And we must master it. For it's our only path to the promised land of creating wide consensus behind wise policy.

Here's my theory: for the first hundred and sixty years of this experiment in democracy that we call America, it was the federal level of government that rendered us unique. The Founding Fathers' singular idea (if you read David McCullough's recent masterpiece, "John Adams," you learn that it was founding mothers as well, for Abigail Adams gave as much to the revolution as her husband) of an activist government assisting an aspirational people, was what set us apart.

That era ended with the death of Franklin Roosevelt in 1945. By then, the industrial age and complexities of modern life rendered unworkable the idea of remote Washington bureaucrats making decisions that affect our health, education, and well-being, and we entered the age of states being the indispensable government level.

State governments became the innovative, flexible place for reforming the uniquely American manner of self-government. This era peaked with the 1979 publication of David Osborne's "Laboratories of Democracy," an examination of those states reforming public education, health, and welfare. The book's introduction was written by a young, ambitious Arkansas governor named Bill Clinton.

I believe that the state government era ended twelve years ago, and today local government is our nation's most important level and, indeed, where all the action is. Look around. In the past five years, Los Angeles adopted a minimum wage standard that's higher than that in the rest of California. In Minnesota, thanks to the work of Myron Orfield and others, localities require affluent suburban school districts to share resources, responsibilities, and yes, revenue, with their city district. And just a few hour drive from here, in Ohio, you can drive into a town or village and at the border they'll stop you and ask, "do you have any handguns because we don't allow handguns in our town."

The point is that today local governments are entering into functions and duties that heretofore were the purview of state and federal governments. That's new, that's exciting, that's an opportunity.

As a result, it seems to me, in this new century, the promise of democracy shall be redeemed one city and one region at a time. This new age will produce several American urban success stories. And I believe that there's no reason on God's earth why Buffalo should not be among them.

Here's my point: the American city, how it's financed, sustained, and for what it stands, is about to be reinvented. And the long-term answer to what ails us lies not in Albany or Washington, but rather right here among us in these affluent suburbs which surround us. Our city's on fire. The hose and water with which we can douse it is in our suburbs.

We caused this problem, and together now, we're going to solve it. But to accomplish this, we must embrace a new community spirit that beckons every Western New Yorker, throughout every suburb, to recognize Buffalo's essential role in our future, and commit to sustaining it.

And I submit to you that this cause is noble; our abilities, great; and our interests, common and united.

In this spirit, permit me to respectfully offer one specific step that you might consider to fully engage in this exciting challenge. I think Buffalo State should establish an advocacy center for regional reform. We all know that over at UB John Sheffer and Kate Foster and the Institute of Local Governance do a great job as a clearinghouse for information. But it's not enough. With the tasks ahead, we need an impartial, academic-based institution that forcefully advances equitable sharing of resources and responsibilities across city-suburban lines.

And its offices should be downtown. There's a gaping hole caused by the absence of any academic institution housed in our downtown government district surrounding City Hall, the Rath Building and Old County Hall. Students would benefit immensely from being in the center of government activity, and Buffalo State should consider filling the hole.

Here's my point: in this new age in which we find ourselves, old standards of knowledge, ability, profession, and most important, civic obligation, have increased. For businessmen and entrepreneurs, it's not enough anymore to write checks and attend political fundraisers. For politicians, it's not enough to have their horizon end at their district's boundary. For educators, it's not enough to even think about town and gown, because today they've become one. And for students, it's not enough to sit on the sidelines in places reserved, as Francis Bacon wrote, only for God and his angels.

In this age of inclusive and cooperative governance, no man, no woman, no government, not church, no citizen, and now no college, can be an island.

And do you know why? Because too many new challenges beckon. How long in this new century do you think America can sustain let alone rationalize itself when growing disparities — not just between us and a people halfway around the world, but as well between folks who live four blocks east of here and those who live ten blocks north — make us a lesser people?

And that's why I've undertaken these several initiatives to which Dr. Howard kindly referred, to encourage us to view governance, education, and spirituality as one. And together, to aspire to something larger than ourselves.

The bad news is, I think I should continue in this work. The worse news is, I think you should undertake it as well. As Americans, when it comes time to make an accounting of ourselves, in addition to the other questions posed, I believe that some divine entity shall ask, "You were an American. You were free. What did you do with your freedom? Did you use it to make other people free?"

One of my heroes is Sam Adams. Now there was a maverick. Among an exceptional generation, he stood out with exceptional courage. He wouldn't brook hesitation, and he wouldn't give the Brits one inch. But ironically, his best pal was a Tory loyalist, and each afternoon, they would walk along the Charles River and discuss matters of the day. In the course of one conversation about Britain and America, Adams later wrote, " it was not until I mentioned the word revolution that I saw my friend's knees buckle."

As Americans and Western New Yorkers, the idea of radical change doesn't make our knees buckle, but rather our pulse race, our minds quicken, and our hearts soar. In our collective struggle to keep our nation and our city forever young, we recognize the essential nature of changing the old. And I believe that in this generation, those with the courage to effect change will find themselves with companions in every corner of this region.

So this morning, in this season of Ramadan, Christmas lights, and Hebrew candles, we think of the six Western New Yorkers whose souls were among the thousands given over for God and nation last September. And with every effort we make to build a city and region worthy of their memory, we feel their presence, and whisper their names.

And as the second year of this new century draws to a close, we also give thanks. For the remarkable news is that we made it. Of all American cities, perhaps no other was treated more unkind by the last century than ours. As Langston Hughes' character, "Simple," once exclaimed, "I have been shot, stabbed, wounded, held down, shut in, locked out, under fed, under paid, under loved, and everything but undertaken. But I am still here."

Well, we're all still here. And we say let's give birth to America's first city without boundaries right here, right now. In this nation or world, there's no place like us, no sense of place to match us. Here, where eastern sophistication meets mid-western charm, we have a thrilling story to tell.

It's a humane story. It's a heroic story. It's a fragile, resilient, redemptive, and ultimately triumphant story. It's the Buffalo story. And once again now, let's tell and re-tell it to ourselves, our children, our nation, and the world.

And as we do, let us pledge ourselves this day to a new civic religion of community renewal, and in one voice pray: as it was in its beginning, it is now, and forever shall be, Buffalo without end, amen.

Thank you very much. ❖

# BIBLIOGRAPHY AND SELECTED READINGS

Among the many gifts my civic work has given me — in addition to collaborating with public servants and scholars throughout America — are the books I've read in the course of my government reform education. Regional thinkers share many qualities, including kindred spirit, quick humor, and fierce community devotion. But perhaps their most admirable trait is a readiness to recommend books, and even shove them into your hands. Some of the authors cited here, I'm proud to call friends. They've been kind enough to share in my work, and several have presented at one or more of my conferences. (For a copy of any final conference report, please send me an e-mail at KevinPGaughan@aol.com.)

In preparing the history essays, I consulted primary and secondary research material, in addition to biographical reading. Ralph Waldo Emerson said that there is no history, only biography, and my lifelong reading habits reflect his assertion. Stories of women and men of great purpose and achievement have always provided inspiration for my work.

In the history section, in addition to the works I consulted, I include books published after I wrote my essays (David McCullough's *John Adams*, for example, which treats the Adams-Jefferson friendship and their final days in new detail). These additional books are all magnificent reads, and they add fresh insight into matters on which I focused.

## REGIONALISM; SPRAWL; URBAN PLANNING; GOVERNMENT AND EDUCATION REFORM; AND COMMUNITY RENEWAL

Bazerman, Max H., Baron, Jonathan, and Shonk, Katherine, *You Can't Enlarge the Pie: Six Barriers to Effective Government.* Cambridge: Basic Books, 2001.

Dodge, William R., *Regional Excellence.* Washington, DC: National League of Cities, 1996.

Duany, Andres, Plater-Zyberk, Elizabeth, and Speck, Jeff, *Suburban Nation: The Rise of Sprawl and the Decline of the American Dream.* New York: North Point Press, 2000.

Grogan, Paul S., and Proscio, Tony, *Comeback Cities*. Boulder: Westview Press, 2000.

Heifetz, Ronald A., *Leadership Without Easy Answers*. Cambridge: Harvard University, 1998.

Hughes, Mark Alan, and Steinberg, Julie E., *The New Metropolitan Reality: Where the Rubber Hits the Road in Anti-Poverty Policy*. Washington, DC: Urban Institute, 1992.

Kaplan, Robert D., *An Empire Wilderness: Travels into America's Future*. New York: Random House, 1998.

Katz, Bruce, ed., *Reflections on Regionalism*. Washington, DC: Brookings Institution, 2000.

Kozol, Jonathan, *Savage Inequalities*. New York: Crown Publishers, 1991.

_____, *Amazing Grace*. New York, Crown Publishers, 1995.

Kunstler, James Howard, *The Geography of Nowhere: The Rise and Decline of America's Man-Made Landscape*. New York: Simon and Schuster, 1993.

_____, *Home From Nowhere: Remaking Our Everyday World for the Twenty-First Century*. New York: Simon and Schuster, 1996.

Loeb, Paul Rogat, *Soul of a Citizen*. New York: St. Martin's Griffin, 1999.

Magnet, Myron, *The Millennial City: A New Urban Paradigm for 21ˢᵗ Century America*. Chicago: Irving R. Dee, 2000.

Mother Theresa, *In My Own Words*. New York: Gramercy Books, 1996.

Orfield, Myron, *Metropolitics: A Regional Agenda for Community and Stability*. Washington, DC: Brookings Institution and Lincoln Institute of Land Policy, 1997.

Peirce, Neal R., Johnson, Curtis W., and Hall, John Stuart, *Citistates: How Urban America Can Prosper in a Competitive World*. Washington, DC; Seven Locks Press, 1993.

Peirce, Neal R. and Johnson, Curtis W., *Boundary Crossers*. College Park: Academy of Leadership Press, 1997.

Rosenblatt, Roger, *Where We Stand: 30 Reasons for Loving Our Country*. New York: Harcourt, 2002.

Rusk, David, *Cities Without Suburbs*, 2d. ed. Johns Hopkins University Press, 1995.

_____, *Inside Game Outside Game: Winning Strategies for Saving Urban America*. Washington, DC: Brookings Institution Press, 1999.

Varady, David P., Preiser, Wolfgang F. E., Russell, Francis P., ed. *New Directions in Urban Public Housing*. New Brunswick: RutgersUniversity Press, 1998.

## NEWSPAPERS AND PERIODICALS

Broder, David, "Look What Happened to the Neighborhood." The Washington Post (April 23, 1997): A-21.

Carney, Paul, "Charter Schools and CDC's." Internal Memorandum, Local Initiatives Support Corporation, September 9, 1998.

Firestone, David, "Suburban Comforts Thwart Atlanta's Plans to Limit Sprawl." New York Times (November 21, 1999): A-1.

Fulton, William, "Seeing the Regional Future." Governing Magazine (April 1999).

Hershberg, Theodore, "New Standards in Education: A Regional Approach to Human Capital Development." The Regionalist, Vol.2, No. 4, Winter 1997.

_____, "The Case for New Standards in Education." Education Week, 1-4, December 1997.

_____, "Teacher Accountability Conference Pre-Conference Report." Center for Greater Philadelphia, April 2000.

Katz, Bruce, "Divided We Sprawl." Atlantic Monthly (December 1999).

Orfield, Gary, "In Pursuit of a Dream Deferred: Linking Housing and Education; Metropolitan School Desegregation; Impacts on Metropolitan Society." Minnesota Law Review 80 (April 1996).

Porter, Michael, "New Strategies for Inner City Economic Development."Economic Development Quarterly 11, No. 1 (February 1997).

Radin, Charles A., "A Neighborhood Re-born." Boston Globe Magazine (November 15, 1998): 12.

Whelan, Charles, "Turning the Table on School Choice." New York Times (May 25, 1999): A-27.

## HISTORY

Adler, Selig and Connolly, Thomas E., From Ararat to Suburbia:The History of the Jewish Community of Buffalo. Philadelphia: 1960.

Allison, John Murray, Adams and Jefferson: the Story of a Friendship. Norman, Oklahoma: Oklahoma Press, 1966.

Ambrose, Stephen, D Day: June 6, 1944: The Climatic Battle of World War II. New York: Simon and Schuster, 1994.

_____, Undaunted Courage: Meriwether Lewis, Thomas Jefferson, and the Opening of the American West. New York: Simon and Schuster, 1996.

Anderson, Floyd, Father Baker. Milwaukee, 1960.

Armitrage, C.H., Cleveland As Buffalo Knew Him. Buffalo: 1927.

Begin, Menachem, The Revolt: Story of the Irgun. New York: H. Schuman, 1951.

Beschloss, Michael, The Crisis Years: Kennedy and Krushchev, 1960-1963. New York: Simon and Schuster, 1991.

Bowman, John, *De Valera and the Ulster Question, 1917-1973*.  Oxford, England: Clarendon Press,1982.

Bradley, James, *Flags Of Our Fathers*.  New York: Bantam, 2000.

Brody, Fawn, *Thomas Jefferson: An Intimate History*.  New York:  Scribner, 1974.

Brookhiser, Richard, *Alexander Hamilton*.  New York: Touchstone, 1999.

Burrows, Edwin G., and Wallace, Mike, *Gotham: A History of New York City to 1898*.  New York: Oxford University Press, 1999.

Butterfield, L.H., Friedlander, Marc, and Kline, Mary Jo, ed., *The Book of Abigail and John: Selected Letters of the Adams Family*.  Cambridge: Harvard University Press, 1966.

Cahill, Kevin, *How the Irish Saved Civilization*.  New York: Doubleday, 1995.

Chesman, G. Wallace, *Governor Theodore Roosevelt*.  Cambridge:  Harvard University Press, 1965.

Coogan, Tim Pat, *Eamonn De Valera: The Man Who Was Ireland*.  Colorado: Roberts Rinehart, 1993.

_____, *Michael Collins: The Man Who Made Ireland*.  Boulder: Roberts Rinehart, 1996.

Donald, David Herbert, *Lincoln*.  New York: Simon and Schuster, 1995.

Eban, Abba, *Personal Witness: Israel Through My Eyes*.  New York:1992.

Editors of American Heritage Magazine, *The Erie Canal*.  New York:  American Heritage Press, 1964.

Ellis, Joseph J., *Passionate Sage: The Character and Legacy of John Adams*. New York: Norton, 1993.

_____, *American Sphinx*.  New York: Alfred. A. Knopf, 1997.

Flexner, James Thomas, *Washington: The Indispensable Man*.  New York: Penguin, 1969.

Foote, Shelby, *Stars In Their Courses: The Gettysburg Campaign*.  New York: Random House, 1963.

Gottlieb, Robert and Kimball, Robert, eds., *Reading Lyrics*.  New York: Pantheon Press, 2000.    Jefers, H. Paul, *Colonel Roosevelt Goes To War*.  New York: Crown Books, 1996.

Jenkins, Roy, *Churchill*.  New York: Farrar Straus Giroux, 2001.

Kunhardt, Phillip B., Jr., Kunhardt, Phillip B. III, and Kunhardt, Peter W., *Lincoln: An Illustrated Biography*.  New York: Random House, 1992.

Malone, Dumas, *Jefferson and the Ordeal of Liberty*.  New York: Little, Brown, 1962.

McCullough, David, *Mornings On Horseback*.  New York: Simon and Schuster, 1981.

_____, *Truman*.  New York: Simon and Schuster, 1992.

_____, *John Adams*.  New York: Simon and Schuster, 2001.

Morris, Edmund, *The Rise of Theodore Roosevelt*. New York: Ballantine, 1979.

_____, *Theodore Rex*. New York: Random House, 2001.

Morris, Jan, *Lincoln: A Foreigner's Quest*. New York: Simon and Schuster, 2000.

Moris, Elting E. and Blum, John, ed., *The Letters of Theodore Roosevelt* Cambridge: Harvard University Press, 1951-4.

Nowlan, Kevin B. and O'Connell, Maurice R., ed., *Daniel O'Connell: Portrait of a Radical*. New York: Fordham University Press, 1985.

Percival, John, *The Great Famine: Ireland's Potato Famine, 1845-1851*. London: 1995.

Renehan, Edward J. Jr., *The Lion's Pride: Theodore Roosevelt and His Family in Peace and War*. New York: Oxford University Press, 1998.

Roosevelt, Theodore, *The Rough Riders*. New York, 1899.

Rybczynski, Witold, *A Clearing in the Distance: Frederick Law Olmsted and America in the Nineteenth Century*. New York: Scribner, 1999.

Sheriff, Carol, *The Artificial River*. New York: Farrar Straus Giroux, 1996.

Sorensen, Theodore, *Kennedy*. New York: Bantam, 1966.

Ward, Geoffrey C., *Before the Trumpet: Young FDR*. New York: Harper and Row, 1985.

_____, *A First-Class Temperament: The Emergence of FDR*. New York: Harper and Row, 1989.

Winik, Jay, *April 1865*. New York: Harper Collins, 2001.

Wister, Owen, *Roosevelt: The Story of a Friendship*. New York, 1930.

## PRIMARY MATERIAL AND SOURCES

Roosevelt's Rough Riders Association: By Laws and Membership, 1912. (Copy No. 454). Housed in the closed stack archives of the Buffalo and Erie County Public Library.

Severance, Frank H., ed., Millard Fillmore Papers. Buffalo Historical Society Publications. Volume 10. 1907.

The Buffalo News. Microfilm editions for July 1898 and October 1898. Buffalo and Erie County Public Library.

The Theodore Roosevelt Collection, Harvard College, Houghton Library, Cambridge, Massachusetts. Includes several letters of TR written from Buffalo, New York (some on Iroquois Hotel letterhead) at various times in his life.